MW01616588

10,000 Legal words

For Secretaries, Stenographers, Typists, Court Reporters, and Students

Compiled by Margaret A. Kurtz
Colby Sawyer College
New London, New Hampshire

Dorothy Adams
Colby Sawyer College
New London, New Hampshire

Jeannette Vezeau, C.S.C., Ph.D.
President, Notre Dame College
Manchester, New Hampshire

McGraw-Hill Book Company

*New York St. Louis San Francisco Auckland Bogotá Guatemala Hamburg
Johannesburg Lisbon London Madrid Mexico Montreal New Delhi
Panama Paris San Juan São Paulo Singapore Sydney Tokyo Toronto*

Other McGraw-Hill wordbooks:

10,000 Medical Words by Edward E. Byers
20,000 Words, Seventh Edition, by Louis A. Leslie

First McGraw-Hill Trade Edition, 1984

2 3 4 5 6 7 8 9   BKPBKP   8 7 6 5

ISBN 0-07-035645-9

10,000 LEGAL WORDS

Library of Congress Catalog Card Number 74-154230

ISBN: 0-07-035645-9

Foreword

Secretaries, stenographers, typists, court reporters, and all others whose work or training for work involves the preparation of legal documents and correspondence often encounter the problem of correctly spelling and dividing words not commonly used outside the legal profession. The purpose of *10,000 Legal Words* is to provide the user with a convenient reference for spelling and dividing legal terms, as well as some of the more troublesome everyday words.

THE WORD LIST

The list of more than 10,000 words and phrases in this book includes a number of legal terms not shown in either the abridged or the unabridged editions of ordinary dictionaries. In all instances possible, however, the spelling and the syllabication of words in this reference have been checked to assure agreement with *Webster's Seventh New Collegiate Dictionary,* 1970 printing (published by G. & C. Merriam Company, Springfield, Massachusetts). The spelling and the syllabication of words not shown in that dictionary have been checked against other dictionaries as well as various source documents and publications.

Selection of Vocabulary. The vocabulary has been very carefully selected from transcripts of court cases, general and technical dictionaries, and other sources to assure that the word list comprises the most commonly used legal words and phrases. Thus the word list includes:

- The 971 legal terms that appeared most often in 3,948 letters dictated by 101 lawyers, as reported by Jeannette Vezeau, C.S.C., in her unpublished doctoral dissertation, "A Study of Legal Terminology Pertinent to the Educational Preparation of the Legal Secretary'' (Boston University, Boston, Massachusetts, 1960).

- The legal terms found in the transcripts of seven complete cases concerning domestic relations, tax evasion, accident insurance, probate and administration of an estate, formation and management of a corporation, equity, and importation and concealment of narcotics.
- The highly technical legal terms appearing in glossaries supplied by law offices, as well as many similar words and phrases appearing in such technical dictionaries as *Black's Law Dictionary* (published by West Publishing Company, St. Paul, Minnesota), and *Legal Secretary's Concise Dictionary* (published by Claitor's Book Store, Baton Rouge, Louisiana).
- Approximately 500 foreign legal words and phrases selected because of their frequent use or because of their helpfulness in expressing accepted legal concepts. Included, for example, are the names of writs (such as *supersedeas*), the names of pleas (such as *semper paratus*), and the more commonly used expressions (such as *ad hoc, bona fide,* and *ex post facto*).
- Those medical terms often used in court cases involving insurance claims, sanity hearings, and work-connected pathological conditions. Among these are terms designating medical specialists who may be called for expert testimony in such cases.

Derivative Forms. Many derivative forms are included in the word list because it is frequently the derivative rather than the original word that poses a problem to the user. Forms like *referred* and *referring,* for example, are given.

Homonyms. A number of homonyms and similar frequently confused words are listed with brief definitions to help the user decide quickly which word should be used in a particular situation; for example, *minor* (*one under legal age*) and *miner* (*mine worker*). These definitions obviously are not meant to be complete—they are simply clues to meaning.

Compound Words and Phrases.   Should the expression be written as one word, as two words, or with a hyphen? Since this is a question that the user must answer often, the word list includes many compound words and phrases: *postdate, post hoc, post-obit,* and so on.

THE REFERENCE SECTION

The reference section following the word list in this book provides a variety of punctuation rules for the person preparing legal documents and correspondence. These rules are illustrated with excerpts from legal materials. The user whose work often involves special problems naturally will require a more complete presentation of rules, such as that in the *Reference Manual for Stenographers and Typists, Fourth Edition,* by Ruth E. Gavin and William A. Sabin (published by Gregg Division, McGraw-Hill Book Company, New York). In addition, the user may require technical references such as *Legal Secretary's Complete Handbook* by Besse May Miller (published by Prentice-Hall, Inc., Englewood Cliffs, New Jersey) and *Manual for the Legal Secretarial Profession* (published by West Publishing Company, St. Paul, Minnesota).

Margaret A. Kurtz
Dorothy Adams
Jeannette Vezeau, C.S.C.

In This Book

The division of words into syllables is indicated by a centered period.

    ab·ju·ra·tion   am·or·tiz·a·ble

Because the typist never breaks off a one-letter syllable, at either the beginning or the end of a word, such syllables are not indicated.

    *a*bridg·ment   ad·ver·sary

Syllables of two or more letters are indicated, although the typist rarely breaks off a syllable of less than three letters. However, printers often break off syllables of two letters.

    co·sig·na·to·ry   in·her·it·ed

Words whose syllabication or spelling varies with their use as different parts of speech are identified by the abbreviation *n.* (noun), *v.* (verb), *adj.* (adjective), *adv.* (adverb), and so on.

    pre·sent v.   pres·ent adj., n.

Homonyms and other words that are often confused are followed by a short "clue" definition and, where appropriate, *cf.* (meaning "compare").

    ad·vice n. (information;   ad·vise v. (inform;
        cf. *advise*)   cf. *advice*)

A

ab·ac·tion
ab·ac·tor
ab·alien·ate
aban·don
aban·doned
aban·don·ee
aban·don·er
aban·don·ing
aban·don·ment
aban·dun *or*
  aban·dum *or*
  aban·don·um
ab an·te
aba·sia
aba·tare
abate
abate·able
abat·ed
abate·ment
abat·er
aba·tu·da
ab·bre·vi·ate
ab·bre·vi·at·ing
ab·bre·vi·a·tion
ab·bre·vi·a·tor
ab·broch·ment *or*
  ab·broach·ment
ab·di·ca·ble
ab·di·cate

ab·di·ca·tion
ab·di·ca·tor
ab·di·tor·i·um
ab·duct
ab·duct·ed
ab·duc·tion
ab·duc·tor
abear·ance
ab·er·ra·tion
ab·er·ra·tion·al
abet
abet·ment
abet·ted
abet·ting
abet·tor *or*
  abet·ter
ab ex·tra
abey·ance
  (suspension; cf.
  obeyance)
abey·ant
abide
abid·ed
abid·er
abil·i·ty
ab in·i·tio
ab·in·tra
abish·er·ing *or*
  abish·er·sing
ab·ju·di·ca·tio
ab·ju·ra·tion
ab·jure
ab·jur·er
ab·lo·ca·tio
ab·ne·gate
ab·ne·ga·tion

ab·ne·ga·tor
abode
abol·ish·able
abol·ish·er
abol·ish·ment
ab·o·li·tion
ab·o·li·tion·ary
ab·o·li·tion·ism
ab·o·li·tion·ist
abort
abor·ti·fa·cient
abor·tion
abor·tion·al
abor·tion·ist
abor·tive
abor·tive·ly
abor·tive·ness
above—en·ti·tled
abra·sion
abridg·able
abridge
abridged
abridg·er
abridg·ment *or*
  abridge·ment
ab·ro·ga·ble
ab·ro·gate
ab·ro·gat·ed
ab·ro·ga·tion
ab·ro·ga·tive
ab·ro·ga·tor
ab·scond
ab·scond·ed
ab·scond·er
ab·sence
ab·sent

ab·sen·tee
ab·sen·tee·ism
ab·sent·ly
ab·so·lute
ab·so·lute·ly
ab·so·lute·ness
ab·so·lu·tion
ab·so·lut·ism
ab·solv·able
ab·solve
ab·sol·vent
ab·solv·er
ab·solv·ing
ab·sorb·able
ab·sorbed
ab·sor·bent
ab·sorb·er
abs·que hoc
áb·stract
ab·stract·ed·ly
ab·stract·ed·ness
ab·strac·tion
ab·stract·ly
ab·stract·ness
ab·strac·tor *or*
    ab·stract·er
abuse
abused
abus·er
abu·sive
abu·sive·ly
abu·sive·ness
abut·ment
abut·tal
abut·ted
abut·ter

abut·ting
ac·a·dem·ic
acad·e·my
ac·cede (agree; cf.
    exceed)
ac·ced·ed
ac·ced·ence
ac·cel·er·ate
ac·cel·er·a·tion
ac·cel·er·a·tive
ac·cept (take;
    cf. *except*)
ac·cept·abil·i·ty
ac·cept·able
ac·cept·able·ness
ac·cept·ably
ac·cept·ance
ac·cept·ed
ac·cep·tor *or*
    ac·cept·er
ac·cess (admittance;
    cf. *excess*)
ac·ces·si·bil·i·ty
ac·ces·si·ble·ness
ac·ces·si·bly
ac·ces·sion
ac·ces·sion·al
ac·ces·so·ri·ly
ac·ces·so·ri·ness
ac·ces·so·ry
ac·ci·dent
ac·ci·den·tal
ac·ci·den·tal·ly
ac·com·mo·date
ac·com·mo·dat·ed
ac·com·mo·dat·ing

ac·com·mo·da·tion
ac·com·mo·da-
    tion·al
ac·com·mo·da·tive
ac·com·mo·da-
    tive·ness
ac·com·pa·nied
ac·com·pa·ny
ac·com·pa·ny·ing
ac·com·plice
ac·cord
ac·cor·dance
ac·cor·dant
ac·cor·dant·ly
ac·cord·ing·ly
ac·couche·ment
ac·count·abil·i·ty
ac·count·able
ac·count·able·ness
ac·coun·tant
ac·cred·it
ac·cred·i·ta·tion
ac·crete
ac·cre·tion
ac·cre·tion·ary
ac·cre·tive
ac·cru·al
ac·crue
ac·crued
ac·crue·ment
ac·cru·ing
ac·cu·mu·late
ac·cu·mu·la·tion
ac·cu·mu·la·tive·ly
ac·cu·mu·la·tor
ac·cus·al

ac·cu·sa·tion
ac·cu·sa·tive
ac·cu·sa·tive·ly
ac·cu·sa·to·ry
ac·cuse
ac·cused
ac·cus·er
ac·cus·ing·ly
ac·cus·tomed
ac·knowl·edge
ac·knowl·edge·able
ac·knowl·edged
ac·knowl·edged·ly
ac·knowl·edg·ing
ac·knowl·edg·ment
a con·trar·io
ac·quaint
ac·quaint·ance·ship
ac·quaint·ed
ac·quest
ac·qui·esce
ac·qui·es·cence
ac·qui·es·cent·ly
ac·quir·able
ac·quire·ment
ac·qui·si·tion
ac·quis·i·tive·ness
ac·quit
ac·quit·tal
ac·quit·tance
ac·quit·ted
ac·quit·ter
ac·quit·ting
acre·age
ac·tio ci·vil·is
ac·tion·able

ac·tion·ably
ac·tio·nes in
  per·so·nam
ac·tion
  ex con·trac·tu
ac·tion
  ex de·lic·to
ac·tio
  per·so·nal·is
ac·tu·al
ac·tu·al·i·ty
ac·tu·al·iza·tion
ac·tu·al·ize
ac·tu·al·ly
ac·tu·ar·i·al
ac·tu·ar·i·al·ly
ac·tu·ary
ac·tu·ate
ac·tu·a·tion
ac·tu·a·tor
ac·tum
ac·tus Dei
ad ab·sur·dum
adapt (adjust; cf.
  adept, adopt)
adapt·abil·i·ty
adapt·able
ad·ap·ta·tion
ad·ap·ta·tion·al
adapt·ed
adapt·er *or*
  adapt·or
adap·tive·ly
a da·tu
ad cu·ri·am
ad dam·num

ad·den·da pl.
ad·den·dum sing.
ad·dict
ad·dict·ed
ad·dic·tion
ad·dic·tive
ad·di·tion (increase;
  cf. *edition*)
ad·di·tion·al
ad·di·tion·ales
ad·di·tion·al·ly
ad·di·tur
ad·dled
ad·dling
ad·dress·ee
ad·duce
ad·duc·er
ad·duc·i·ble
ad·duct
adeem
ademp·tion
ad·ept (skillful; cf.
  adapt, adopt)
ad·e·qua·cy
ad·e·quate·ly
ad·e·quate·ness
ad fa·cien·dum
ad fi·lum aq·uae
ad fi·nem
ad·here
ad·her·ence
ad·her·ent
ad·he·sion
ad hoc
ad idem
adieu sing.

adieus *or*
  adieux pl.
ad in·fi·ni·tum
ad in·ter·im
ad·i·tus
ad·ja·cen·cy
ad·ja·cent·ly
ad·join·ing
ad·journ
ad·journed
ad·journ·ment
ad·judge
ad·ju·di·cate
ad·ju·di·cat·ed
ad·ju·di·cat·ee
ad·ju·di·ca·tion
ad·ju·di·ca·tive
ad·ju·di·ca·tor
ad·ju·di·ca·to·ry
ad·junct
ad·junc·tion
ad·junc·tive
ad·junct·ly
ad·ju·ra·tion
ad·jure
ad·just·able
ad·just·ed
ad·just·er
ad·just·ment
ad·just·men·tal
ad li·bi·tum
ad li·tem
ad lo·cum
ad·mea·sure·ment
ad·min·is·ter
ad·min·is·tered

ad·min·is·tra·ble
ad·min·is·trant
ad·min·is·trate
ad·min·is·tra·tion
ad·min·is·tra·tive
ad·min·is·tra·tor
ad·min·is·tra·trix
  fem.
ad·mi·ral·ty
ad·mis·si·bil·i·ty
ad·mis·si·ble
ad·mis·sion
ad·mis·sive
ad·mit·tance
ad·mit·ted
ad·mit·ted·ly
ad·mit·ting
ad·mix·ture
ad·mon·ish
ad·mon·ished
ad·mon·ish·er
ad·mon·ish·ing·ly
ad·mon·ish·ment
ad·mo·ni·tion
ad·mon·i·to·ry
ad·o·les·cence
ad·o·les·cent
adopt (accept; cf.
  adapt, adept)
adopt·abil·i·ty
adopt·able
adopt·er
adop·tion
adop·tive
ad quod
  dam·num

ad rem
ad res·pon·den·dum
adroit·ly
ad·ses·sores
adult
adul·ter·ate
adul·ter·a·tion
adul·ter·a·tor
adul·ter·er
adul·ter·ess
adul·ter·ine
adul·ter·ous·ly
adul·tery
adult·hood
ad va·lo·rem
ad·vance
ad·vanced
ad·vanc·es
ad·vance·ment
ad·ven·ti·tious·ly
ad·ven·ti·tious·ness
ad·ven·ture
ad·ven·tur·er
ad·ven·tur·ism
ad·ven·tur·ist
ad·ven·tur·is·tic
ad·ver·sary
ad·verse
  (unfavorable; cf.
  averse)
ad·verse·ly
ad·verse·ness
ad·ver·si·ty
ad·ver·sus
ad·ver·tise·ment

ad·vice n. (informa-
  tion; cf. *advise*)
ad·vis·abil·i·ty
ad·vis·able
ad·vis·able·ness
ad·vis·ably
ad·vise v. (inform; cf.
  advice)
ad·vised
ad·vis·ed·ly
ad·vise·ment
ad·vis·er or
  ad·vi·sor
ad·vi·so·ri·ly
ad·vi·so·ry
ad vi·tam
ad·vo·ca·cy
ad·vo·cate
ad·vo·cat·ing
ad·vo·ca·tion
ad·vo·ca·tor
af·fect (influence; cf.
  effect)
af·fect·ed·ly
af·fec·tion
af·fec·tion·ate·ly
af·fi·ance
af·fi·ant
af·fi·da·vit
af·fil·i·ate
af·fil·i·at·ed
af·fil·i·a·tion
af·fin·age
af·fin·i·ty
af·firm·able
af·fir·mance

af·fir·mant
af·fir·ma·tion
af·fir·ma·tive·ly
af·fix
af·fix·a·tion
af·fixed
af·flict·ed
af·flic·tion
af·force
af·for·est
af·for·es·ta·tion
af·fran·chise
af·fray
af·freight·ment
af·front
afore·men·tioned
afore·said
afore·thought
a for·ti·o·ri
af·ter—ac·quired
af·ter—
  dis·cov·ered
af·ter·math
af·ter·thought
af·ter·ward
agen·cy
agen·da pl.
agen·dum sing.
ag·gra·vate
ag·gra·vat·ed
ag·gra·va·tion
ag·gre·gate
ag·gre·gate·ly
ag·gre·gat·ing
ag·gre·ga·tio
  men·tium

ag·gre·ga·tion
ag·gre·ga·tive
ag·gress
ag·gres·sion
ag·gres·sive·ly
ag·gres·sive·ness
ag·gres·sor
ag·grieve
ag·grieved
agist·er or
  agis·tor
agist·ment
ag·i·tate
ag·i·ta·tion
ag·i·ta·tor
ag·nate
ag·nat·ic
ag·nat·i·cal·ly
ag·na·tion
ag·o·nize
ag·o·ny
agrar·i·an
agree·able
agreed
agree·ing
agree·ment
ag·ri·cul·tur·al·ist
ag·ri·cul·tur·al·ly
ag·ri·cul·ture
ail·ment
air·craft
air force
air·plane
air·port
air·strip
air·way

al·co·hol·ic
al·co·hol·i·cal·ly
al·co·hol·ism
al·der·man
ale·ato·ry
alias (pl.: *aliases*)
alias dic·tus
alias·es (sing.: *alias*)
al·i·bi
al·i·bied
al·i·bi·ing
alien·abil·i·ty
alien·able
alien·age
ali·e·na res
alien·ate
alien·at·ed
alien·ation
alien·ator
alien·ee
ali·e·ni ju·ris
alien·ism
alien·ist
alien·or
align·er
align·ment
al·i·mo·ny
al·i·quot
al·i·ter
al·i·un·de
al·lay (soothe; cf. *alley, ally*)
al·le·ga·ta et pro·ba·ta
al·le·ga·tion
al·lege

al·leged
al·leg·ed·ly
al·leg·es
al·le·giance
al·leg·ing
al·ler·gy
al·ley (passage; cf. *allay, ally*)
al·ley·way
al·li·ance
al·lo·ca·ble
al·lo·cat·able
al·lo·cate
al·lo·cat·ed
al·lo·ca·tion
al·lo·cu·tion
al·lo·graph·ic
al·longe
al·lo·path·ic
al·lo·path·i·cal·ly
al·lot
al·lot·ment
al·lot·ted
al·lot·tee
al·lot·ting
al·low·able
al·low·ance
al·lowed (permitted; cf. *aloud*)
al·lude (refer to; cf. *elude*)
al·lud·ed
al·lu·sion (reference; cf. *elusion, illusion*)
al·lu·sive
al·lu·vi·on

al·ly (associate; cf. *allay, alley*)
aloud (audibly; cf. *allowed*)
al·ter v.
al·ter·abil·i·ty
al·ter·able
al·ter·ably
al·ter·ation
al·ter·ca·tion
al·ter ego
al·ter·nate
al·ter·na·tive·ly
alum·na sing. fem.
alum·nae pl. fem.
alum·ni pl. mas.
alum·nus sing. mas.
a ma·jo·ri ad mi·nus
amal·ga·ma·tion
amal·ga·ma·tive
am·bas·sa·dor
am·bas·sa·do·ri·al
am·bas·sa·dor·ship
am·bi·gu·i·ty
am·big·u·ous·ly
am·big·u·ous·ness
am·bit
am·bu·lance
am·bu·la·to·ry
am·bush
am·bush·ment
ame·lio·rate
ame·lio·ra·tion
ame·lio·ra·tor
ame·lio·ra·to·ry

ame·na·ble
ame·na·bly
amend·able
amen·da·to·ry
amend·ed
amende
  ho·no·ra·ble
amend·er
amend·ment
ame·ni·ty
a men·sa et
  tho·ro
amerce
amerced
amerce·ment
amer·cia·ble
am·i·ca·bil·i·ty
am·i·ca·ble
am·i·ca·bly
ami·cus cu·ri·ae
am·ne·sia
am·nes·ty
am·or·tiz·a·ble
amor·ti·za·tion
am·or·tize
amo·tion
am·pli·a·tion
am·pli·fi·ca·tion
am·pli·fy
am·pu·tate
am·pu·tat·ed
am·pu·ta·tion
anal·o·gous·ly
anal·o·gous·ness
an·a·logue *or*
  an·a·log

anal·o·gy
anal·y·ses pl.
anal·y·sis sing.
an·a·lyt·ic
an·a·lyt·i·cal
an·a·lyt·i·cal·ly
an·a·lyze
an·a·lyz·er
an·aph·ro·di·sia
an·aph·ro·dis·i·ac
an·ar·chism
an·ar·chist
an·ar·chy
anat·o·cism
an·a·tom·i·cal
anat·o·my
an·ces·tor
an·ces·tral·ly
an·ces·tress
an·ces·try
an·chor
an·chor·age
an·chored
an·chy·lo·sis *or*
  an·ky·lo·sis
an·cient
an·cient·ly
an·cient·ness
an·cil·lary
an·es·the·sia
an·es·the·si·ol·o-
  gist
an·es·thet·ic
anes·the·tize
an·eu·rysm
an·eu·rys·mal

an·gi·na pec·to·ris
an·guish
an·guished
an·i·mo
  con·tra·hen·di
an·i·mo et ac·ta
an·i·mos·i·ty
an·i·mus fu·ran·di
an·i·mus
  re·ver·ten·di
an·i·mus
  tes·tan·di
an·nex·a·tion
an·nexed
an·ni·ver·sa·ry
an·no Do·mi·ni
an·no·tate
an·no·tat·ed
an·no·ta·tion
an·no·ta·tor
an·nounce·ment
an·nounc·er
an·noy·ance
an·noyed
an·noy·er
an·noy·ing·ly
an·nu·al·ly
an·nu·itant
an·nu·ities pl.
an·nu·ity sing.
an·nul
an·nul·able
an·nulled
an·nul·ling
an·nul·ment
anom·a·lous

7

anom·a·lous·ly
anom·a·lous·ness
anom·a·ly
an·o·nym·i·ty
anon·y·mous·ly
an·swer
an·swer·able
an·swered
an·swer·er
an·te
an·te·cede
an·te·ced·ence
an·te·ced·ent
an·te·ced·ent·ly
an·te·ces·sor
an·te·date
an·te   li·tem
an·te   mor·tem
an·te·na·tal
an·ten·na   sing.
an·ten·nae   or
   an·ten·nas   pl.
an·te·nup·tial
an·ti·bi·ot·ic
an·ti·chre·sis
an·tic·i·pate
an·tic·i·pat·ed
an·tic·i·pa·tion
an·tic·i·pa·tive·ly
an·tic·i·pa·tor
an·tic·i·pa·to·ry
an·ti·dote
an·tig·ra·phy
an·ti·mo·ny
an·ti·sep·tic
an·ti·so·cial

an·ti·trust
apart·ment
apart·men·tal
apha·sia
apha·sic
apho·nia
apol·o·gize
apol·o·gy
ap·o·plec·tic
ap·o·plec·ti·cal·ly
ap·o·plexy
a   pos·te·ri·o·ri
apoth·e·cary
ap·pa·ra·tus   sing.
ap·pa·ra·tus·es   pl.
ap·par·el
ap·par·eled   or
   ap·par·elled
ap·par·ent·ly
ap·peal·abil·i·ty
ap·peal·able
ap·pealed
ap·peal·er
ap·pear·ance
ap·peared
ap·pel·lant
ap·pel·late
ap·pel·lee
ap·pel·lor
ap·pend
ap·pen·dage
ap·pen·dant
ap·pend·ed
ap·pen·dix   sing.
ap·pen·dix·es   or
   ap·pen·di·ces   pl.

ap·per·tain·ing
ap·pli·ance
ap·pli·ca·bil·i·ty
ap·pli·ca·ble
ap·pli·ca·bly
ap·pli·cant
ap·pli·ca·tion
ap·pli·ca·tive
ap·pli·ca·tor
ap·plied
ap·pli·er
ap·ply·ing
ap·point·ed
ap·poin·tee
ap·point·ive
ap·point·ment
ap·poin·tor
ap·por·tion
ap·por·tioned
ap·por·tion·ment
ap·prais·al
ap·praise   (value; cf.
   apprise)
ap·praised
ap·praise·ment
ap·prais·ers
ap·prais·ing·ly
ap·pre·cia·ble
ap·pre·cia·bly
ap·pre·ci·ate
ap·pre·ci·at·ed
ap·pre·ci·a·tion
ap·pre·cia·to·ry
ap·pre·hend
ap·pre·hend·ed
ap·pre·hen·si·ble

ap·pre·hen·si·bly
ap·pre·hen·sion
ap·pre·hen·sive
ap·pre·hen·sive-
  ness
ap·pren·tice·ship
ap·prise (inform; cf.
  appraise)
ap·prised
ap·proach
ap·proach·abil·i·ty
ap·proach·able
ap·pro·pri·a·ble
ap·pro·pri·ate
ap·pro·pri·at·ed
ap·pro·pri·ate·ly
ap·pro·pri·ate·ness
ap·pro·pri·a·tion
ap·pro·pri·a·tive
ap·pro·pri·a·tor
ap·prov·able
ap·prov·ably
ap·prov·al
ap·prove
ap·prov·er
ap·prov·ing·ly
ap·prox·i·mate
ap·prox·i·mate·ly
ap·prox·i·ma·tion
ap·prox·i·ma·tive
ap·pur·te·nance
ap·pur·te·nant
a pri·o·ri
ap·ro·pos
aquat·ic
aq·uo

ar·a·ble
ar·bi·ter
ar·bi·trage
ar·bit·ra·ment
ar·bi·trar·i·ly
ar·bi·trar·i·ness
ar·bi·trary
ar·bi·trate
ar·bi·trat·ed
ar·bi·trat·ing
ar·bi·tra·tion
ar·bi·tra·tion·al
ar·bi·tra·tive
ar·bi·tra·tor
ar·che·type
ar·chi·tect
ar·chi·tec·tur·al·ly
ar·chi·tec·ture
ar·chi·val
ar·chives
ar·chi·vist
area·way
ar·gen·tum
ar·gu·able
ar·gue
ar·gu·en·do
ar·gu·ing
ar·gu·ment
ar·gu·men·ta·tion
ar·gu·men·ta·tive
  or ar·gu·men-
  tive
ar·gu·men·tum
ar·pen·ta·tor
ar·raign (charge; cf.
  arrange)

ar·raigned
ar·raign·ment
ar·range (order; cf.
  arraign)
ar·ranged
ar·rang·er
ar·range·ment
ar·ray
ar·rear·age
ar·rears
ar·rect (accuse; cf.
  erect)
ar·rest
ar·rest·ed
ar·rest·er *or*
  ar·res·tor
ar·rest·ment
ar·ret·ted
ar·riv·al
ar·ro·gate
ar·ro·ga·tion
ar·se·nal
ar·son·ist
ar·ti·cle
ar·ti·cling
ar·tic·u·late
ar·tic·u·lat·ed
ar·tic·u·late·ly
ar·tic·u·late·ness
ar·tic·u·la·tion
ar·tic·u·la·tive
ar·tic·u·la·tor
ar·tic·u·la·to·ry
ar·tic·u·lo mor·tis
ar·ti·fice
ar·ti·fi·cer

ar·ti·fi·cial
ar·ti·fi·ci·al·i·ty
ar·ti·fi·cial·ly
as·cend
as·cend·able *or*
as·cend·ible
as·cen·dan·cy *or*
as·cen·den·cy
as·cen·dant
as·cend·ed
as·cend·er
as·cent (climb; cf.
assent)
as·cer·tain·a·ble
as·cer·tain·a·bly
as·cer·tained
as·cer·tain·ment
as·crib·able
as·cribe
as·pect
as·perse
as·per·sion
as·per·sive
as·phyx·ia
as·phyx·i·ate
as·phyx·i·a·tion
as·phyx·i·a·tor
as·por·ta·tion
as·por·ta·tor
as·sail
as·sail·able
as·sail·ant
as·sailed
as·sas·sin
as·sas·si·nate
as·sas·si·nat·ed

as·sas·si·nat·ing
as·sas·si·na·tion
as·sault
as·sault·ed
as·sault·er
as·say
as·say·er
as·sem·blage
as·sem·ble
as·sem·bled
as·sem·bler
as·sem·bly
as·sem·bly·man
as·sent (approval; cf.
ascent)
as·sent·ed
as·sen·tor
as·sert·ed
as·ser·tion
as·sert·ive·ly
as·sert·ive·ness
as·ser·to·ry
as·sess
as·sess·able
as·sessed
as·sess·ment
as·ses·sor
as·set
as·sign·able
as·sign·ably
as·signed
as·sign·ee
as·sign·er *or*
as·sign·or
as·sign·ment
as·sist

as·sis·tance
as·sis·tant
as·sist·ed
as·size
as·so·ci·ate v.
as·so·ciate n.
as·so·ci·at·ed
as·so·ci·at·ing
as·so·ci·a·tion
as·so·cia·tive
as·soil
as·soil·ment
as·sume
as·sumed
as·sum·ing
as·sump·sit
as·sump·tion
as·sump·tive
as·sur·ance
as·sure
as·sured·ly
as·sured·ness
astip·u·la·tion
as·ti·tu·tion
asy·lum
atax·ia
athe·ism
athe·ist
athe·is·tic
athe·is·ti·cal·ly
atro·cious·ly
atro·cious·ness
atroc·i·ty
atroph·ic
at·ro·phied
at·ro·phy

at·ro·phy·ing
at·tach·able
at·tached
at·tach·ment
at·tain
at·tain·abil·i·ty
at·tain·able·ness
at·tain·der
at·taint
at·tempt
at·tempt·able
at·tempt·ed
at·tend
at·ten·dance
at·ten·dant
at·tend·ed
at·ten·tion
at·ten·tive·ly
at·test
at·test·ant
at·tes·ta·tion
at·test·ed
at·test·er
at·torn
at·tor·ney
  gen·er·al
at·tor·neys
  gen·er·al *or*
   at·tor·ney
  gen·er·als
at·tor·ney·ship
at·torn·ment
at·tract·ed
at·trac·tion
at·trac·tive·ly
at·trac·tive·ness

at·trib·ut·a·ble
at·tri·bute n.
at·trib·ute v.
at·trib·ut·ed
at·trib·ut·er
at·tri·bu·tion
at·trib·u·tive·ly
atyp·i·cal
atyp·i·cal·ly
au con·traire
auc·tion
auc·tioned
auc·tion·eer
au·di·ence
au·dit
au·dit·ed
au·di·tor
aus·cul·ta·tion
au·then·tic
au·then·ti·cal·ly
au·then·ti·cate
au·then·ti·cat·ed
au·then·ti·cat·ing
au·then·ti·ca·tion
au·then·ti·ca·tor
au·then·tic·i·ty
au·thor·i·ta·tive·ly
au·thor·i·ta·tive-
  ness
au·thor·i·ties
au·thor·i·ty
au·tho·ri·za·tion
au·tho·rize
au·tho·rized
au·tho·riz·er
au·to·crat·ic

au·to·crat·i·cal·ly
au·to·graphed
au·to·mate
au·to·mat·ed
au·to·mat·ic
au·to·mat·i·cal·ly
au·to·ma·tion
au·tom·a·tism
au·tom·a·ti·za·tion
au·tom·a·tize
au·to·mo·bile
au·to·mo·tive
au·ton·o·mist
au·ton·o·mous·ly
au·ton·o·my
au·top·sies
au·top·sy
aux·il·ia·ries
aux·il·ia·ry
avail·abil·i·ty
avail·able
avail·ably
aver
av·er·age
av·er·age·ness
aver·ment
averred
aver·ring
averse (disinclined;
  cf. *adverse*)
averse·ly
averse·ness
aver·sion
avi·a·tion
a vin·cu·lo
  mor·tis

11

av·o·ca·tion (hobby; cf. *vocation*)
avoid·able
avoid·ably
avoid·ance
avoid·ed
av·oir·du·pois
avouch
avouched
avouch·er
avouch·ment
avow·al
avow·ant
avowed
avowed·ly
avow·ee
avow·er
avow·ry
avul·sion
award·ed
ax·i·om
ax·i·om·at·ic
ax·i·om·at·i·cal·ly

B

back·ward·ly
back·ward·ness
bade (commanded)
bag·gage

bail (release)
bail·able
bailed
bail·ee
bai·liff
bail·liff·ship
bail·ment
bail·or
   or bail·er
bails·man
bal·ance
bal·anced
bal·anc·er
bal·last
bal·last·age
bal·lis·tic
bal·lis·tics
bal·lot
bal·lot·ed
bal·lot·er
bal·lot·ing
ban·dage
ban·daged
ban·dit
ban·dit·ry
ban·ish
ban·ished
ban·ish·er
ban·ish·ment
bank·able
bank check
bank·er
bank·rupt
bank·rupt·cy
bar·gain
bar·gained

bar·gain·er
barge
bar·ra·tor   *or*
   bar·ra·ter
bar·ra·trous
bar·ra·try
barred
bar·rel
bar·reled
   or bar·relled
bar·rel·ing
   or bar·rel·ling
bar·ren·ly
bar·ren·ness
bar·ri·cade
bar·ri·cad·ed
bar·ri·er
bar·ring
bar·ris·ter
bar·ter
bar·tered
bar·ter·er
base·less
bas·es (pl. of *base* and *basis*; cf. *basis*)
ba·sis (foundation; cf. *bases*)
bas·tard
bas·tard·iza·tion
bas·tard·ize
bas·tard·ly
bas·tardy n.
bat·tery
bat·ture
bay·ou
bea·con

bear·able
bear·ably
bear·er
bed·ded
bed·ding
beg·gar·ing
be·gin·ner
be·gin·ning
be·got·ten
be·half
be·have
be·haved
be·hav·ior
be·hav·ior·al·ly
be·hooves
be·lief
be·liev·able
be·lieve
be·lieved
bel·lig·er·ence
bel·lig·er·en·cy
bel·lig·er·ent
be·long
be·longed
bene·fac·tor mas.
bene·fac·tress fem.
ben·e·fi·cial·ly
ben·e·fi·ciar·ies
ben·e·fi·ciary
ben·e·fit
ben·e·fit·ed
    or ben·e·fit·ted
ben·e·fit·ing
    or ben·e·fit·ting
be·nev·o·lence
be·nev·o·lenc·es

be·nev·o·lent·ly
be·nev·o·lent·ness
be·nign
be·queath
be·queath·al
be·queathed
be·quest
be·rate
be·rat·ed
be·seech
be·seeched
be·sides
be·sot
be·sot·ted
be·sot·ting
be·sought
be·stow
be·stow·al
be·stowed
be·tray
be·tray·al
be·trayed
be·tray·er
be·tray·ing
be·troth·al
be·trothed
bet·ter (good; cf. *bettor*)
bet·tered
bet·ter·ment
bet·tor (gambler; cf. *better*)
bev·er·age
bi·an·nu·al (twice a year; cf. *biennial*)
bi·an·nu·al·ly

bi·as
bi·ased *or* bi·assed
bi·as·ing *or* bi·as·sing
bi·as·ness
bid·da·bil·i·ty
bid·da·ble
bid·den
bid·der
bid·ding
bi·en·ni·al (once in two years; cf. *biannual*)
bi·en·ni·al·ly
bi·en·ni·um
big·a·mist
big·a·mous·ly
big·a·my
big·ot
big·ot·ed·ly
big·ot·ry
bi·lat·er·al
bi·lat·er·al·ism
bi·lat·er·al·ly
bi·lat·er·al·ness
bilged
billed (charged; cf. *build*)
bill·er
bil·let
bind·er
bi·o·log·ic
bi·o·log·i·cal·ly
bi·op·sy
bi·zarre adj.

13

black·jack
black·list
black·mail
black·mailed
black·mail·er
blam·able
blame·less
blank   check
blank
   en·dorse·ment
blan·ket
blas·pheme
blas·phem·er
blas·phe·mous·ly
blas·phe·my
block·ade
block·ad·ed
block·ad·er
block·ade—run·ner
blood·hound
blood·shed
blood·stained
blood   test
blud·geon
blud·geoned
blue   law
blue·print
blue   rib·bon n.
blue—rib·bon adj.
blue—sky adj.
bluff
blun·der
blun·dered
blun·der·er
board·er
board·ing·house

bod·i·ly
bo·gus
bois·ter·ous·ly
bois·ter·ous·ness
bona   fide
bona   fi·des
bo·na   va·can·tia
bond·able
bond·ed
bond·er
bonds·man
bon·i·fi·ca·tion
bo·nus
book·keep·er
book·mak·er
boot·leg
boot·legged
boot·leg·ger
boot·leg·ging
boo·ty
bor·row
bor·rowed
bor·row·er
bot·tle
bot·tled
bot·tle·neck
bot·tling
bot·tom·ry
bot·u·lism
bou·doir
bounce
bounc·er
bound·a·ries
bound·a·ry
boun·ty
bour·geois

bour·geoi·sie
bourse
boy·cott
brain·wash
branch·es
brand·ed
brand·er
bran·dish
bran·dished
bra·va·do
brawl
bra·zen·ly
breach
breached
breach·es
break·able
break·age
break   down v.
break·down n.
brew·ery
brib·able
bribe
bribed
brib·er
brib·er·ies
brib·ery
brief
brief·less
brig·and
bro·ken
bro·ker
bro·ker·age
broth·el
bruise
bruised
bruis·er

14

bru·tal
bru·tal·i·ty
bru·tal·iza·tion
bru·tal·ize
bru·tal·ly
bud·get
bud·get·ary
bud·get·ed
bud·ge·teer
  or bud·get·er
buff·er
build (construct; cf.
  billed)
build·er
bul·let
bul·le·tin
bul·let·proof
bull·head·ed·ly
bull·head·ed·ness
bul·lion (gold)
bull·pen
bun·dle
bun·dled
bun·dling
bun·gle
bun·gled
bun·gling
buoy·an·cy
buoy·ant
bur·den
bur·dened
bur·den·some
bur·den·some·ness
bu·reau
bu·reau·cra·cy
bu·reau·crat

bur·glar
bur·glar·ize
bur·gla·ry
buri·al
bur·sar
busi·ness
but·tals
buy·er
by·law *or*
  bye·law
by·pass n., v.
by—prod·uct
by·stand·er

cab·a·ret
cab·driv·er
cab·i·net
ca·boose
cache
ca·dav·er
ca·dav·er·ic
ca·dav·er·ous·ly
ca·det
ca·du·ca
ca·du·ca·ry
ca·gey
ca·hoots
ca·jole

ca·joled
ca·jol·ery
ca·lam·i·tous·ly
ca·lam·i·tous·ness
ca·lam·i·ty
cal·ci·fi·ca·tion
cal·ci·fied
cal·ci·fy·ing
cal·cu·la·bil·i·ty
cal·cu·la·ble
cal·cu·late
cal·cu·lat·ed
cal·cu·lat·ing
cal·cu·la·tion
cal·cu·la·tor
cal·en·dar (time)
cal·en·dared
cal·lous
ca·lum·ni·ate
ca·lum·ni·a·tion
ca·lum·ni·a·tor
ca·lum·ni·ous·ly
cal·um·ny
cam·bist
cam·bist·ry
cam·ou·flage
cam·paign
cam·paigned
cam·paign·er
can·cel
can·celed *or*
  can·celled
can·cel·er *or*
  can·cel·ler
can·cel·ing *or*
  can·cel·ling

15

can·cel·la·tion
can·di·da·cy
can·di·date
can·did·ly
can·did·ness
can·dor
can·na·bis
can·non (weapon; cf. *canon, canyon*)
can·on (accepted rule; cf. *cannon, canyon*)
can·vas n. (cloth)
can·vass v. (solicit)
can·vassed
can·vass·er
can·vass·ing
can·yon (ravine; cf. *cannon, canon*)
ca·pa·bil·i·ty
ca·pa·ble·ness
ca·pa·bly
ca·pac·i·ty
ca·pi·as ad sa·tis·fac·ien·dum
cap·i·la·tion
ca·pi·ta (sing.; *caput*)
cap·i·tal (city, property; cf. *capitol*)
cap·i·tal·ism
cap·i·tal·ist
cap·i·tal·is·tic
cap·i·tal·is·ti·cal·ly
cap·i·tal·iza·tion
cap·i·tal·ize
cap·i·tol (building; cf. *capital*)

ca·pit·u·late
ca·pit·u·lat·ed
ca·pit·u·la·tion
cap·tain
cap·tain·cy
cap·ta·tor
cap·tion
cap·tioned
cap·tive
cap·tiv·i·ty
cap·tor
cap·ture
cap·tured
ca·put (pl.: *capita*)
car·cass
car·ci·no·gen·ic
car·ci·no·ma
car·di·ol·o·gist
car·dio·vas·cu·lar
care·less·ly
care·less·ness
car·go sing.
car·goes *or* car·gos pl.
car·nal
car·nal·i·ty
car·nal·ly
car·ried
car·ri·er
car·ry·ing
car·tel
car·ti·lage
case law
case·work·er
cash·ier
cas·ket

ca·su·al·ly
ca·su·al·ness
ca·su·al·ties
ca·su·al·ty
ca·sus for·tu·i·tus
ca·tas·tro·phe
cat·a·stroph·ic
cat·a·stroph·i·cal·ly
cat·e·gor·i·cal·ly
Cau·ca·sian
cau·cus
cau·sa
caus·al
cau·sal·i·ty
caus·al·ly
cau·sa mor·tis
cau·sa prox·i·ma
cau·sa qua su·pra
cau·sa se·cun·da
cau·sa sine qua non
cau·sa·tion
caus·ative·ly
cau·sa·tor
cause·less
cau·tion
cau·tion·ary
cau·tioned
cau·tious
cau·tious·ly
cau·tious·ness
ca·ve·at ac·tor
ca·ve·at emp·tor
cease
ceased

cease·less·ly
cease·less·ness
cease—fire n.
cede (yield)
ced·ed
ced·er
ce·ler·i·ty
cel·i·ba·cy
cel·i·bate
cel·lar (storeroom; cf. *seller*)
ce·ment
ce·ment·ed
ce·ment·er
ce·ment·ing
cem·e·tery
cen·sor·ship
cen·sur·able
cen·sure
cen·sured
cen·sur·er
cen·sus (count; cf. *senses*)
cen·tral·i·ty
cen·tral·iza·tion
cen·tral·ize
cen·tral·ly
ce·re·bral
ce·re·bro·spi·nal
cer·tain·ly
cer·tain·ty
cer·ti·fi·able
cer·ti·fi·ably
cer·tif·i·cate
cer·ti·fi·ca·tion
cer·tif·i·ca·to·ry

cer·ti·fied
cer·ti·fi·er
cer·ti·fies
cer·ti·fy
cer·ti·fy·ing
cer·tio·ra·ri
ces·sion (yielding; cf. *session*)
ces·sion·ary
cess·ment
ces·sor *or* ces·ser
ces·sure
ces·tui que trust
ces·tui que use
ces·tui que vie
chaf·fery
chal·lenge
chal·lenged
chal·leng·er
cham·bered
cham·bers
cham·fer
cham·per·ty
cham·pi·on
chan·cel·lor·ship
chan·cery
chan·nel
chan·neled *or* chan·nelled
chan·nel·iza·tion
chan·nel·ize
chap·el
chap·lain·cy
chap·lain·ship
char·ac·ter

char·ac·ter·is·tic
char·ac·ter·is·ti·cal·ly
char·ac·ter·iza·tion
char·ac·ter·ize
char·ac·ter·less
charge·able
charge·able·ness
charged
charg·er
char·i·ta·ble·ness
char·i·ta·bly
char·i·ty
char·la·tan
char·la·tan·ism
char·la·tan·ry
char·ter
char·tered
char·ter·er
chas·sis
chaste (virtuous)
chaste·ness
chas·ti·ty
chat·tel
chau·cer
chau·cery
chauf·feur
check·book
check·point
check·up n.
check up v.
chem·i·cal
child·birth
child·hood
child·ish·ly
child·ish·ness

chi·ro·prac·tic
chi·ro·prac·tor
choose (select)
chose (selected)
chose in ac·tion
Chris·tian
Chris·tian·i·ty
chron·ic
chron·i·cal·ly
chro·nic·i·ty
chro·no·log·ic
chro·no·log·i·cal·ly
chro·nol·o·gy
cir·ca
cir·cuit
cir·cu·itous
cir·cu·lar·iza·tion
cir·cu·lar·ize
cir·cu·late
cir·cu·lat·ed
cir·cu·lat·ing
cir·cu·la·tion
cir·cu·la·tor
cir·cum·lo·cu·tion
cir·cum·scribe
cir·cum·scribed
cir·cum·scrib·ing
cir·cum·scrip·tion
cir·cum·spect
cir·cum·spec·tion
cir·cum·stance
cir·cum·stan·ti·al-
  i·ty
cir·cum·stan·tial·ly
cir·cum·stan·ti·ate
cir·cum·vent·ed

cir·cum·vent·ing
cir·cum·ven·tion
ci·ta·tion
cite (refer; cf. *sight,*
  site)
cit·ed
cit·i·zen·ship
civ·ic
civ·il
ci·vil·ian
ci·vi·li·ter
  mor·tu·us
ci·vil·i·ty
civ·i·li·za·tion
civ·i·lize
claim·able
claim·ant
claimed
claim·er
clan·des·tine
clan·des·tine·ly
clar·i·fi·ca·tion
clar·i·fied
clar·i·fy
clar·i·fy·ing
clar·i·ty
clas·si·fi·able
clas·si·fi·ca·tion
clas·si·fied
clas·si·fi·er
clas·si·fy
clas·si·fy·ing
clause
claus·es
clear·ance
cleared

clear·ing·house
clem·en·cy
clem·ent·ly
cler·gy·man
cler·i·cal·ly
clerk·ship
cli·ent
cli·ent·age
cli·en·tal adj.
cli·en·tele n.
close—hauled
clo·ture
co·ad·ju·tor
co·ad·min·is·trate
co·ad·min·is·tra-
  tion
co·ad·min·is·tra·tor
co·ad·ven·ture
co·ad·ven·tur·er
co·ali·tion
co·ali·tion·ist
co·as·sign·ee
coc·cyx
co·coun·sel
co·de·fen·dant
cod·i·cil
cod·i·cil·la·ry
co·di·fi·ca·tion
cod·i·fied
cod·i·fy
cod·i·fy·ing
co·emp·tion
co·equal
co·equal·ly
co·erce
co·erced

co·erc·ible
co·erc·ing
co·er·cion
co·er·cive
co·er·cive·ness
co·ex·ec·u·tor
cog·nate
cog·nate·ly
cog·na·tion
cog·ni·za·ble
cog·ni·za·bly
cog·ni·zance
cog·ni·zant
cog·no·men sing.
cog·no·mens or
 cog·no·mi·na pl.
cog·nom·i·nal
co·hab·it
co·hab·i·tant
co·hab·i·ta·tion
co·heir
co·heir·ess
coin·age
co·ition
co·ition·al
co·ital
co·itus
col·lab·o·rate
col·lab·o·rat·ed
col·lab·o·ra·tion
col·lab·o·ra·tion-
 ism
col·lab·o·ra·tion·ist
col·lab·o·ra·tive
col·lab·o·ra·tor
col·lapse

col·lapsed
col·laps·ibil·i·ty
col·laps·ible
col·late
col·lat·ed
col·lat·er·al
col·lat·er·al·i·ty
col·lat·er·al·ly
col·lat·ing
col·la·tion
col·la·tor
col·lect·ed·ly
col·lect·ed·ness
col·lect·ible
 or col·lect·able
col·lec·tion
col·lec·tive·ly
col·lec·tor
col·lide
col·lid·ed
col·li·sion (accident;
 cf. collusion)
col·lo·cate
col·lo·ca·tion
col·lu·sion (agree-
 ment; cf. collision)
col·lu·sive·ly
col·o·ny
col·or·able
col·or·ation
co·ma·ker
co·ma·tose
com·bat·ed
 or com·bat·ted
com·bat·ing
 or com·bat·ting

com·bi·na·tion·al
com·bine
com·fort·able
com·fort·ably
com·fort·ed
com·i·ty
com·mand (order; cf.
 commend)
com·man·dant
com·mand·ed
com·man·deer
com·mand·er
com·mand·ment
com·mence
com·menced
com·menc·ing
com·mend (praise;
 cf. command)
com·men·da·tion
com·mend·ed
com·men·su·rate
com·ment
com·men·tary
com·merce
com·mer·cial
com·mer·cial·ism
com·mer·cial·ist
com·mer·cial·is·tic
com·mer·cial·iza-
 tion
com·mer·cial·ize
com·mer·cial·ly
com·min·gle
com·mi·nute
com·mi·nut·ed
com·mi·nu·tion

com·mis·sion
com·mis·sioned
com·mis·sion·er
com·mis·sive
com·mit
com·mit·ments
com·mit·ta·ble
com·mit·tal
com·mit·ted
com·mit·tee·man
com·mit·tee·wom·an
com·mit·ting
com·mit·ti·tur
com·mix
com·mix·tion
com·mix·ture
com·mod·i·ties
com·mod·i·ty
com·mon·ly
com·mon·ness
com·mon·wealth
com·mo·ran·cy
com·mo·rien·tes
com·mo·tion
com·mu·nal
com·mu·nal·ism
com·mu·nal·ist
com·mu·nal·i·ty
com·mu·nal·ize
com·mune
com·mu·ni·ca·ble
com·mu·ni·cate
com·mu·ni·cat·ed
com·mu·ni·ca·tion
com·mu·ni·ca-
  tive·ly

com·mu·ni·ca·tor
com·mu·nism
com·mu·nist
com·mu·nis·tic
com·mu·nis·ti·cal·ly
com·mu·ni·ty
com·mut·able
com·mu·tate
com·mu·ta·tion
com·mut·ta·tive
com·mu·ta·tiv·i·ty
com·mu·ta·tor
com·mute
com·mut·ed
com·pact
com·pact·ly
com·pact·ness
com·pac·tor
  or com·pact·er
com·pa·nies
com·pan·ion·ship
com·pa·ny
com·pa·ra·bil·i·ty
com·pa·ra·ble·ness
com·pa·ra·bly
com·par·a·tive·ly
com·pared
com·par·i·son
com·part·ment
com·pas·sion
com·pas·sion·ate·ly
com·pat·i·bil·i·ty
com·pat·i·ble
com·pat·i·ble·ness
com·pat·i·bly
com·pel

com·pel·la·ble
com·pel·la·tion
com·pelled
com·pel·ler
com·pel·ling
com·pen·di·um sing.
com·pen·di·ums *or*
  com·pen·dia pl.
com·pen·sa·ble
com·pen·sate
com·pen·sat·ed
com·pen·sa·tion
com·pen·sa·tive
com·pen·sa·tor
com·pen·sa·to·ry
com·pete
com·pet·ed
com·pe·tence
com·pe·ten·cy
com·pe·tent·ly
com·pet·ing
com·pe·ti·tion
com·pet·i·tive·ly
com·pet·i·tor
com·pi·la·tion
com·pile
com·piled
com·pil·er
com·plain·ant
com·plained
com·plain·er
com·plain·ing·ly
com·plaint
com·ple·ment
  (amount; cf.
  compliment)

com·ple·men·ta·ry
com·plete
com·plet·ed
com·plete·ly
com·plete·ness
com·ple·tion
com·plex
com·plex·ion
com·plex·i·ty
com·plex·ly
com·plex·ness
com·pli·ance
com·pli·an·cy
com·pli·ant
com·pli·ant·ly
com·pli·cate
com·pli·cat·ed
com·pli·cat·ing
com·pli·ca·tion
com·plic·i·ty
com·plied
com·pli·ment
   (congratulate; cf.
   complement)
com·pli·men·ta·ry
com·ply·ing
com·pose
com·posed
com·pos·ite
com·pos·ite·ly
com·po·si·tion
com·po·si·tion·al
com·pos men·tis
com·po·sure
com·pound
com·pound·able

com·pound·ed
com·pound·er
com·pre·hend·ed
com·pre·hen·si·ble
com·pre·hen·sion
com·pre·hen·sive·ly
com·prise
com·prised
com·pro·mise
com·pro·mised
com·pro·mis·er
comp·trol·ler·ship
com·pul·sion
com·pul·sive·ly
com·pul·sive·ness
com·pul·so·ry
com·pur·ga·tion
com·pur·ga·tor
com·pu·ta·tion·al
com·pute
com·put·ed
com·put·er
con·ceal
con·ceal·able
con·cealed
con·ceal·ment
con·cede
con·ced·ed
con·ced·ed·ly
con·ceiv·able
con·ceiv·ably
con·ceive
con·cen·trate
con·cen·trat·ed
con·cen·trat·ing
con·cen·tra·tion

con·cept
con·cep·tion
con·cep·tion·al
con·cep·tive
con·cep·tu·al·ly
con·cern
con·cerned
con·cern·ment
con·cert·ed
con·ces·sion
con·ces·sive·ly
con·cil·i·ate
con·cil·i·a·tion
con·cil·i·a·tive
con·cil·i·a·tor
con·cil·ia·to·ry
con·clude
con·clud·ed
con·clud·er
con·clu·sion
con·clu·sive
con·clu·sive·ly
con·clu·sive·ness
con·com·i·tance
con·com·i·tant
con·com·i·tant·ly
con·cord
con·cor·dance
con·cor·dant·ly
con·cu·bi·nage
con·cu·bine
con·cur
con·curred
con·cur·rence
con·cur·rent
con·cur·rent·ly

con·cur·sus
con·cus·sion
con·cus·sive
con·demn
con·dem·na·ble
con·dem·na·tion
con·dem·na·to·ry
con·demned
con·demn·er
  or con·demn·or
con·di·tion
con·di·tion·al
con·di·tion·al·i·ty
con·di·tion·al·ly
con·di·tioned
con·di·tion·er
con·do·min·i·um
con·do·na·tion
con·done
con·doned
con·done·ment
con·don·er
con·duce
con·du·cive
con·duct
con·duct·ed
con·duct·ibil·i·ty
con·duct·ible
con·duc·tor
con·fed·er·a·cy
con·fed·er·ate
con·fed·er·a·tion
con·fer
con·fer·ee
  or con·fer·ree
con·fer·ence

con·fer·en·tial
con·ferred
con·fer·ring
con·fess
con·fessed
con·fess·ing
con·fes·sion
con·fes·sor
con·fi·dant (friend;
  cf. *confident*)
con·fide
con·fid·ed
con·fi·dence
con·fi·dent (sure; cf.
  confidant)
con·fi·den·tial·ly
con·fi·den·tial·ness
con·fi·dent·ly
con·fid·er
con·fid·ing·ly
con·fine
con·fined
con·fine·ment
con·firm
con·firm·abil·i·ty
con·firm·able
con·fir·ma·tion
con·fir·ma·to·ry
con·firmed
con·firm·ed·ly
con·firm·er
con·fir·mor
con·fis·ca·ble
con·fis·cate
con·fis·cat·ed
con·fis·ca·tee

con·fis·ca·tion
con·fis·ca·tor
con·fis·ca·to·ry
con·flict
con·flict·ed
con·flic·tion
con·form
con·formed
con·for·mi·ty
con·front
con·fron·tal
con·fron·ta·tion
con·fuse
con·fused·ly
con·fus·ing·ly
con·fu·sion
con·fu·ta·tion
con·fu·ta·tive
con·fute
con·fut·er
con·gen·i·tal
con·gest·ed
con·ges·tion
con·gre·gate
con·gre·gat·ed
con·gre·ga·tion
con·gre·ga·tor
con·gress
con·gres·sio·nal
con·gres·sio·nal·ly
con·gress·man
con·gress·wom·an
con·jec·tur·al·ly
con·jec·ture
con·jec·tured
con·jec·tur·er

con·ju·gal
con·ju·gal·i·ty
con·ju·gal·ly
con·junct
con·junc·tion
con·junc·tion·al·ly
con·junc·tive·ly
con·nect·ed·ly
con·nec·tion
con·nec·tive·ly
con·niv·ance
con·nive
con·nived
con·niv·er
con·nu·bi·al
con·quest
con·san·guine
con·san·guin·e·ous·ly
con·san·guin·i·ty
con·science
con·sci·en·tious
con·sci·en·tious·ly
con·sci·en·tious-
   ness
con·scio·na·ble
con·scious·ness
con·script·ed
con·scrip·tion
con·sec·u·tive
con·sec·u·tive·ly
con·sec·u·tive·ness
con·sen·su·al
con·sen·su·al·ly
con·sen·sus
con·sent·ed
con·sent·er

con·sen·tient
con·se·quence
con·se·quent
con·se·quen·tial
con·se·quen·tial·ly
con·ser·va·tion
con·ser·va·tive·ly
con·ser·va·tor
con·ser·va·to·ry
con·serve
con·served
con·sid·er·able
con·sid·er·a·bly
con·sid·er·ate
con·sid·er·ation
con·sid·ered
con·sign
con·sign·able
con·sig·na·tion
con·signed
con·sign·ee
con·sign·ment
con·sign·or
con·sist
con·sis·tence
con·sis·ten·cy
con·sis·tent·ly
con·so·la·tion
con·sole
con·soled
con·sol·i·date
con·sol·i·dat·ed
con·sol·i·da·tion
con·so·nant
con·sort
con·sort·ed

con·sor·tia pl.
con·sor·tium sing.
con·spic·u·ous·ly
con·spic·u·ous·ness
con·spir·a·cy
con·spir·a·tor
con·spir·a·to·ri·al·ly
con·spire
con·spired
con·sta·ble
con·stab·u·lary
con·stant·ly
con·state
con·stit·u·en·cy
con·stit·u·ent
con·stit·u·ent·ly
con·sti·tute
con·sti·tut·ed
con·sti·tu·tion
con·sti·tu·tion·al·ist
con·sti·tu·tion·al·i-
   ty
con·sti·tu·tum
con·strain
con·strain·able
con·strained
con·strained·ly
con·straint
con·struct·ing
con·struc·tion
con·struc·tion·al·ly
con·struc·tion·ist
con·struc·tive
con·struc·tive·ly
con·struc·tive·ness
con·strue

con·strued
con·stu·prate
con·sul (government official; cf. *council,* *counsel*)
con·sul·ar
con·sul·ate
con·sul·ship
con·sult
con·sul·tant
con·sul·ta·ry re·sponse
con·sul·ta·tion
con·sul·ta·tive
con·sult·ed
con·sul·tor
con·sume
con·sumed
con·sum·er
con·sum·mate
con·sum·mat·ed
con·sum·mate·ly
con·sum·ma·tion
con·sum·ma·tive
con·sum·ma·tor
con·sum·ma·to·ry
con·sump·tion
con·ta·gion
con·ta·gious
con·ta·gious·ness
con·tango
con·temn
con·tem·ner *or* con·tem·nor
con·tem·plate
con·tem·plat·ed

con·tem·pla·tion
con·tem·pla·tor
con·tem·po·ra·ne·ous
con·tem·po·rary
con·tempt
con·tempt·ible
con·tempt·ibly
con·temp·tu·ous
con·tend·ed
con·tent·ed·ness
con·ten·tion
con·ten·tious
con·ten·tious·ly
con·ten·tious·ness
con·tent·ment
con·ter·mi·nous
con·ter·mi·nous·ly
con·test
con·test·able
con·tes·tant
con·tes·ta·tion
con·test·ed
con·text
con·tex·tu·al
con·tex·tu·al·ly
con·tex·ture
con·ti·gu·ity
con·tig·u·ous
con·tig·u·ous·ly
con·ti·nent
con·ti·nen·tal
con·ti·nen·tal·ly
con·tin·gen·cy
con·tin·gent
con·tin·gent·ly

con·tin·u·al·ly
con·tin·u·ance
con·tin·u·ando
con·tin·u·ant
con·tin·u·a·tion
con·tin·u·a·tive
con·tin·u·a·tor
con·tin·ue
con·tin·ued
con·tin·u·er
con·tin·u·ing
con·ti·nu·ity
con·tin·u·ous
con·tin·u·ous·ly
con·tra·band
con·tra bo·nos mo·res
con·tract
con·tract·ed
con·tract·ing
con·trac·tor
con·trac·tu·al
con·trac·tu·al·ly
con·tra·dict
con·tra·dict·able
con·tra·dict·ed
con·tra·dic·tion
con·tra·dic·tor
con·tra·dic·to·ri·ly
con·tra·dic·to·ry
con·tra·man·da·tum
con·tra pa·cem
con·tra·ri·ety
con·trar·i·ly
con·trar·i·ness
con·trari·wise

con·trary
con·tra·vene
con·tra·vened
con·tra·ven·er
con·tra·ven·tion
con·trib·ute
con·trib·ut·ed
con·trib·ut·ing
con·tri·bu·tion
con·trib·u·tive
con·trib·u·tive·ly
con·trib·u·tor
con·trib·u·to·ry
con·trive
con·trived
con·triv·er
con·triv·ing
con·trol
con·trol·la·ble
con·trolled
con·trol·ler
con·trol·ling
con·tro·ver·sial
con·tro·ver·sial·ism
con·tro·ver·sial·ist
con·tro·ver·sial·ly
con·tro·ver·sies
con·tro·ver·sy
con·tro·vert·er
con·tro·vert·ible
con·tu·ma·cious
con·tu·ma·cy
con·tu·max
con·tu·me·li·ous
con·tu·me·ly
con·tuse

con·tu·sion
con·u·sant
con·u·see
con·u·sor
con·va·lesce
con·va·les·cence
con·va·les·cent
con·va·lesc·ing
con·vene
con·vened
con·ven·er
con·ve·nience
con·ve·nient·ly
con·ven·tion
con·ven·tion·al
con·ven·tion·al·ism
con·ven·tion·al·ist
con·ven·tion·al·i·ty
con·ven·tion·al-
   iza·tion
con·ven·tion·al·ly
con·ver·sance
con·ver·san·cy
con·ver·sant
con·ver·sa·tion·al
con·verse
con·versed
con·verse·ly
con·ver·sion
con·ver·sion·al
con·ver·sion·ary
con·vert·ed
con·vert·er
con·vert·ibil·i·ty
con·vert·ible
con·vert·ibly

con·vey
con·vey·ance
con·vey·anc·er
con·vey·anc·es
con·vey·anc·ing
con·veyed
con·vey·er *or*
   con·vey·or
con·vey·ing
con·vict
con·vict·ed
con·vic·tion
con·vince
con·vinced
con·vinc·er
con·vinc·ing·ly
con·vinc·ing·ness
con·voy
co—op (cooperative)
co·op·er·ate
co·op·er·at·ed
co·op·er·a·tion
co·op·er·a·tive
co·op·er·a·tive·ness
co—opt (preempt)
co—op·ta·tion
co—op·ta·tive
co—op·tion
co—op·tive
co·or·di·nate
co·or·di·nate·ly
co·or·di·na·tion
co·par·ce·nary
co·par·ce·ner
co·part·ners
co·part·ner·ship

copy·right
copy·right·ed
cor·am non
  ju·di·ce
co·re·spon·dent
  (adulterer; cf.
  correspondent)
cor·ner (angle; cf.
  coroner)
cor·ol·lary
cor·o·nary
cor·o·ner (official; cf.
  corner)
cor·po·ra
cor·po·ral
cor·po·ral·i·ty
cor·po·rate
cor·po·rate·ly
cor·po·ra·tion
cor·po·re·al
cor·po·re·al·i·ty
cor·po·re·al·ly
cor·po·re·ity
corps (group)
corpse (dead body)
cor·pus de·lic·ti
cor·pus ju·ris
  ci·vil·is
cor·rect
cor·rec·tion
cor·rec·tion·al
cor·rec·tive
cor·rec·tive·ly
cor·rec·tive·ness
cor·rec·tor
cor·re·late

cor·re·lat·ed
cor·re·la·tion
cor·re·la·tion·al
cor·rel·a·tive
cor·rel·a·tive·ly
cor·re·spond
cor·re·spond·ed
cor·re·spon·dence
cor·re·spon·dent
  (writer; cf.
  corespondent)
cor·rob·o·rate
cor·rob·o·rat·ed
cor·rob·o·ra·tion
cor·rob·o·ra·tive
cor·rob·o·ra·tor
cor·rob·o·ra·to·ry
cor·rupt
cor·rupt·ed
cor·rupt·er *or*
  cor·rupt·or
cor·rupt·ibil·i·ty
cor·rupt·ible
cor·rupt·ibly
cor·rup·tion
cor·rup·tion·ist
cor·rup·tive
cor·rupt·ly
cor·rupt·ness
cor·ti·cal
cor·ti·co·spi·nal
co·sign
co·sig·na·to·ry
co·sign·er
co·stip·u·la·tor
cos·to·chon·dral

co·sure·ties
co·ten·an·cy
co·ten·ants
co·te·rie
coun·cil (group; cf.
  consul, counsel)
coun·cil·lor *or*
  coun·cil·or
  (member of council;
  cf. *counselor*)
coun·cil·lor·ship
coun·cil·man
coun·sel (advise; cf.
  consul, council)
coun·seled *or*
  coun·selled
coun·sel·ing *or*
  coun·sel·ling
coun·sel·or *or*
  coun·sel·lor
  (lawyer; cf.
  councillor)
coun·sel·or·ship
count·able
coun·ter v.
coun·ter·act
coun·ter·at·tack
coun·ter·bal·ance
coun·ter·check
coun·ter·claim
coun·ter·feit
coun·ter·feit·er
coun·ter·mand
coun·ter·mea·sure
coun·ter·of·fer
coun·ter·part

coun·ter·pro·pos·al
coun·ter·sign
coun·ter·sig·na·ture
coun·ter·signed
coun·ter·vail
coun·try
coun·ty
cou·pon
cour·te·sy
court·house
court—mar·tial
court—mar·tialed
court—mar·tial·ing
courts—mar·tial
court·room
cous·in (relative; cf. *cozen*)
cov·e·nant
cov·e·nan·tal
cov·e·nan·tee
cov·e·nant·er
cov·e·nan·tor
cov·en·try
cov·er·age
cov·ered
cov·er·er
co·vert
co·vert·ly
co·vert·ness
cov·er·ture
cov·in
cov·i·nous
cow·ard·ice
cow·ard·li·ness
cow·ard·ly
coxa sing.

cox·ae pl.
cox·al
coz·en (cheat; cf. *cousin*)
coz·en·age
coz·en·er
cra·ni·al
cra·ni·um
cras·sus
cra·zy
cre·anc·er
cre·dence
cre·den·tials
cred·i·bil·i·ty
cred·i·ble (believable; cf. *creditable*)
cred·i·bly
cred·it·abil·i·ty
cred·it·able (worthy; cf. *credible*)
cred·it·able·ness
cred·it·ably
cred·it·ed
cred·i·tor
cre·du·li·ty
cred·u·lous
cred·u·lous·ly
cred·u·lous·ness
cre·mate
cre·mat·ed
cre·ma·tion
cre·ma·tor
cre·ma·to·ri·um sing.
cre·ma·to·ri·ums or cre·ma·to·ria pl.

cre·pus·cu·lum
cri·er
crime
crim·i·nal
crim·i·nal·i·ty
crim·i·nal·ly
crim·i·nate
crim·i·na·tion
crim·i·no·log·i·cal
crim·i·no·log·i·cal·ly
crim·i·nol·o·gist
crim·i·nol·o·gy
crip·ple
crip·pled
crip·pler
crip·pling
cri·te·ria or cri·te·ri·ons pl.
cri·te·ri·on sing.
crit·ic
crit·i·cal
crit·i·cal·i·ty
crit·i·cal·ly
crit·i·cal·ness
crit·i·cism
crit·i·cize
crit·i·cized
crit·i·ciz·ing
crook·ed
crop·per
cross—ac·tion
cross—claim
cross—de·mand
cross— ex·am·i·na·tion

27

cross—ex·am·ine
cross—ex·am·ined
cross—ex·am·in·er
cross—ex·am·in·ing
cross—file
cross—ques·tion
cross—sale
cross sec·tion
cross·walk
cru·el·ly
cru·el·ness
cru·el·ty
cuck·old·ry
cui bo·no
cul—de—sac
cul·mi·nate
cul·mi·nat·ed
cul·mi·nat·ing
cul·mi·na·tion
cul·pa
cul·pa·bil·i·ty
cul·pa·ble
cul·pa·ble·ness
cul·pa·bly
cul·prit
cul·ti·vate
cul·ti·vat·ed
cul·ti·vat·ing
cul·ti·va·tion
cul·ti·va·tor
cum·ber·some
cum tes·ta·mento an·nexo (abbrev.: c.t.a.)
cu·mu·la·tive

cu·mu·la·tive·ly
cu·mu·la·tive·ness
cu·ra·tive·ly
cu·ra·tor mas.
cu·ra·to·ri·al
cu·ra·tor·ship
cu·ra·trix fem.
cur·few
cu·ria
cur·ren·cy
cur·rent·ly
cur·rent·ness
cur·so·ri·ly
cur·so·ry
cur·tail
cur·tailed
cur·tail·er
cur·tail·ing
cur·tail·ment
cus·to·di·al
cus·to·dia le·gis
cus·to·di·an·ship
cus·to·dy
cus·tom·able
cus·tom·ar·i·ly
cus·tom·ary
cus·tom·er
cus·tom·house
cu·ta·ne·ous
cy·cle
cy·clic
cy·cli·cal
cy·cli·cal·ly
cy pres
cyst
cys·tic

dac·ty·log·ra·phy
dag·ger
dai·ly
dam·age
dam·aged
dam·ag·es
dam·ag·ing·ly
dam·na
dam·na·ble
damned (cursed)
dam·ni·fi·ca·tion
dam·ni·fy
damn·ing
dam·num abs·que in·ju·ria
dam·num et in·ju·ria
dam·num fa·ta·le
dan·ger·ous·ly
dan·ger·ous·ness
dar·rein
da·ta (sing.: datum)
da·tion en paie·ment
da·ti·val
da·tive·ly
da·tum (pl.: data)
daugh·ter—in—law
daugh·ters—in—law

28

day·book
day·light
day·time
dead·born
dead·head
dead·line
dead·lock
dead·locked
dead·ly
deal·er
dealt
death·bed
death·blow
death·ly
death·watch
de·bar·ment
de·base
de·based
de·base·ment
de·bas·er
de·bauch
de·bauch·ee
de·bauch·er
de·bauch·ery
de be·ne es·se
de·ben·ture
deb·it
de bo·nis
  as·por·ta·tis
de bo·nis non
  ad·min·i·stra·tis
de bo·nis
  pro·pri·is
de bo·no et
  ma·lo
de·bride·ment

debt·or
de·cap·i·tate
de·cap·i·tat·ed
de·cap·i·ta·tion
de·cease
de·ceased (dead; cf.
  diseased)
de·ce·dent
de·ceit·ful
de·ceit·ful·ly
de·ceit·ful·ness
de·ceiv·able
de·ceive
de·ceived
de·ceiv·er
dc·ceiv·ing·ly
de·cen·cy
de·cent (proper; cf.
  descent, dissent)
de·cep·tion
de·cep·tive
de·cep·tive·ly
de·cep·tive·ness
de·cide
de·cid·ed
de·cid·er
de·ci·sion
de·ci·sive·ly
de·claim
de·claimed
de·claim·er
dec·la·ma·tion
de·clam·a·to·ry
de·clar·ant
dec·la·ra·tion
de·clar·a·to·ry

de·clare
de·clared
de·clar·er
dec·li·na·tion
dec·li·na·tion·al
de·cline
de·clined
de·coct
de·coc·tion
de·com·pose
de·com·posed
de·com·po·si·tion
dec·o·rate
dec·o·rat·ed
dec·o·rat·ing
dec·o·ra·tion
dec·o·ra·tive
dec·o·ra·tive·ly
dec·o·ra·tor
de·co·rum
de·coy
de·cree (command;
  cf. *degree*)
de·creed
de·cree·ing
de·cre·er
de·crep·it·ly
de·crep·i·tude
de·cre·tal
de·cre·tive
de·cre·to·ry
ded·i·cate
ded·i·cat·ed
ded·i·ca·tion
ded·i·ca·tor
ded·i·ca·to·ry

de·di·tion
de·duce
de·duc·ible
de·duct
de·duct·ibil·i·ty
de·duct·ible
de·duc·tion
de·duc·tive·ly
deed
deem
de·face
de·faced
de·face·ment
de·fac·er
de fac·to
de·fal·cate
de·fal·ca·tion
de·fal·ca·tor
de·falk
def·a·ma·tion
de·fam·a·to·ry
de·fame
de·famed
de·fault
de·fault·ed
de·fea·sance
de·fea·si·ble
de·feat
de·feat·ed
de·feat·ism
de·feat·ist
de·fect·ed
de·fec·tion
de·fec·tive·ly
de·fec·tive·ness
de·fec·tor

de·fend
de·fen·dant
de·fend·ed
de·fense
de·fense·less·ly
de·fense·less·ness
de·fens·es
de·fen·si·bil·i·ty
de·fen·si·ble
de·fen·si·bly
de·fen·sive·ly
de·fen·sive·ness
de·fer
def·er·ence (respect;
   cf. *difference*)
de·ferred
de·fer·ring
de·fi·ance
de·fi·ant
de·fi·ant·ly
de·fi·cien·cies
de·fi·cien·cy
de·fi·cient·ly
def·i·cit
de·fied
de·file
de·file·ment
de·fil·er
def·i·nite
def·i·nite·ly
def·i·ni·tion
de·fin·i·tive·ly
de·fin·i·tive·ness
de·flect
de·flect·ed
de·flec·tion

de·flec·tor
de·force·ment
de·for·ciant
de·form
de·formed
de·for·ma·tion
de·for·mi·ty
de·fraud
de·frau·da·tion
de·fraud·ed
de·fraud·er
de·funct
de·fy·ing
de·gen·er·a·cy
de·gen·er·ate
de·gen·er·a·tion
de·gen·er·a·tive
deg·ra·da·tion
de·grade
de·grad·ed
de·grad·er
de gra·tia
de·gree (extent;
   cf. *decree*)
de·hors
de·hy·drate
de·hy·drat·ed
de·hy·dra·tion
de·jer·a·tion
de ju·re
de·late
de·la·tion
de·la·tor
de·lay
de·layed
de·lay·er

del·e·gate
del·e·gat·ed
del·e·ga·tion
de·lete
de·let·ed
del·e·te·ri·ous·ly
del·e·te·ri·ous·ness
de·let·ing
de·le·tion
de·lib·er·ate
de·lib·er·at·ed
de·lib·er·ate·ly
de·lib·er·ate·ness
de·lib·er·at·ing
de·lib·er·a·tion
de·lib·er·a·tive
de·lib·er·a·tive·ly
de·lib·er·a·tor
de·lict
de·lic·tum
de·lim·it
de·lim·i·ta·tion
de·lim·i·ta·tive
de·lim·it·ed
de·lin·quen·cy
de·lin·quent·ly
de·lir·i·ous·ly
de·lir·i·ous·ness
de·lir·i·um
    tre·mens
de·liv·er
de·liv·er·able
de·liv·er·ance
de·liv·ered
de·liv·er·er
de·liv·ery

de·lu·sion
de·lu·sion·al
de·lu·sive
de·lu·sive·ly
de·lu·sive·ness
de·lu·so·ry
de·mand·able
de·mand·ant
de·mand·ed
de·mand·er
de·mea·nor
de·ment·ed
de·ment·ed·ly
de·men·tia
    par·a·lyt·i·ca
de·men·tia
    prae·cox
de·mesne
de·mesn·i·al
de·mise
de·mised
de·moc·ra·cy
dem·o·crat·ic
dem·o·crat·i·cal·ly
de·mol·ish
de·mol·ished
de·mol·ish·ment
de·mo·li·tion
de·mo·li·tion·ist
de·mon·stra·bil·i·ty
de·mon·stra·ble
de·mon·stra·bly
dem·on·strate
dem·on·strat·ed
dem·on·stra·tion
de·mon·stra·tive·ly

de·mon·stra·tive-
    ness
dem·on·stra·tor
de·mor·al·iza·ion
de·mor·al·ize
de·mur (delay)
de·mure (modest)
de·mur·ra·ble
de·mur·rage
de·mur·ral
de·mur·rant
de·murred
de·mur·rer
de·mur·ring
de·ni·able
de·ni·al
de·nied
de·nies
de·nounce
de·nounced
de·nounce·ment
de·nounc·er
de   no·vo
den·tal·ly
den·tist·ry
de·nu·mer·a·tion
de·nun·ci·a·tion
de·nun·ci·a·tive
de·nun·ci·a·to·ry
de·ny·ing·ly
de·part·ment
de·part·men·tal
de·part·men·tal·ize
de·part·men·tal·ly
de·part·ed
de·par·ture

de·pend·abil·i·ty
de·pend·able·ness
de·pend·ably
de·pen·dence
de·pen·den·cy
de·pen·dent
de·pen·dent·ly
de·plet·able
de·plete
de·plet·ed
de·ple·tion
de·ple·tive
de·po·nent
de·port·able
de·por·ta·tion
de·port·ed
de·pose
de·pos·it
de·pos·i·tary (person)
de·pos·it·ed
de·po·si·tion
de·pos·i·tor
de·pos·i·to·ry (place)
de·pot
de prae·sen·ti
de·pra·va·tion (corruption; cf. *deprivation*)
de·praved
de·praved·ly
de·praved·ness
de·pre·cia·ble
de·pre·ci·ate
de·pre·ci·at·ed
de·pre·ci·at·ing·ly

de·pre·ci·a·tion
de·pre·ci·a·tive
de·pre·ci·a·tor
de·pre·cia·to·ry
dep·re·da·tion
de·pre·da·tor
de·pre·da·to·ry
de·press
de·pressed
de·pres·sant
de·press·ing·ly
de·pres·sion
de·pres·sive
de·pres·sor
de·priv·able
de·priv·al
de·pri·va·tion (loss; cf. *depravation*)
de·prive
de·prived
dep·u·ta·tion
de·pute
dep·u·ties
dep·u·tize
dep·u·ty
de·raign
de·rail
de·rail·ment
de·ranged
de·range·ment
der·e·lict
der·e·lic·tion
der·i·va·tion
der·i·va·tion·al
der·i·va·tive
de·rive

de·riv·er
der·ma·ti·tis
der·ma·tol·o·gist
der·o·gate
der·o·ga·tion
de·ro·ga·tive
de·rog·a·to·ri·ly
de·rog·a·to·ry
de·scend
de·scen·dant *or* de·scen·dent
de·scend·ible
de·scent (decline; cf. *decent, dissent*)
de·scribe
de·scribed
de·scrib·er
de·scrip·tion
de·scrip·tio per·so·nae
de·scrip·tive
de·scrip·tive·ly
des·e·crate
des·e·crat·ed
des·e·crat·er *or* des·e·cra·tor
des·e·cra·tion
de·sert v.
des·ert n.
de·sert·ed
de·sert·er
de·ser·tion
des·ic·cant
des·ic·cate
des·ic·ca·tion
de·sic·ca·tive

des·ic·ca·tor
de·sign
des·ig·nate
des·ig·nat·ed
des·ig·na·tion
des·ig·na·tive
des·ig·na·tor
des·ig·na·to·ry
de·signed
de·sign·ed·ly
de·sign·er
de·sign·ment
de·sir·abil·i·ty
de·sir·able·ness
de·sir·ably
de·sired
de son tort
des·patch·es
des·per·a·do sing.
    des·per·a·dos or
    des·per·a·dos pl.
des·per·ate (hopeless;
    cf. disparate)
des·per·ate·ly
des·per·ate·ness
des·per·a·tion
de·spite
de·spite·ful
de·spite·ful·ness
de·spoil
de·spoil·er
de·spoil·ment
des·pot
des·pot·ic
des·pot·i·cal·ly
des·po·tism

des·ti·na·tion
des·tine
des·tined
des·ti·nies
des·ti·ny
des·ti·tute
des·ti·tute·ness
des·ti·tu·tion
de·stroy
de·stroyed
de·stroy·er
de·struct
de·struc·tion
de·struc·tive·ness
de·sue·tude
de·tail
de·tailed
de·tain
de·tained
de·tain·ee
de·tain·er
de·tain·ment
de·tect·ed
de·tec·tion
de·tec·tive
de·tec·tor
de·ten·tion
de·ter
de·te·ri·o·rate
de·te·ri·o·rat·ed
de·te·ri·o·ra·tion
de·te·ri·o·ra·tive
de·ter·ment
de·ter·min·able
de·ter·min·ably
de·ter·mi·nant

de·ter·mi·nate
de·ter·mi·nate·ly
de·ter·mi·nate·ness
de·ter·mi·na·tion
de·ter·mine
de·ter·mined
de·terred
de·ter·rence
de·ter·rent
de·ter·ring
det·i·nue
de·tour
de·toured
de·tourne·ment
de·tract
de·tract·ed
de·trac·tion
de·trac·tive·ly
de·trac·tor
det·ri·ment
det·ri·men·tal
det·ri·men·tal·ly
de·tur dig·ni·ori
dev·as·tate
dev·as·tat·ed
dev·as·tat·ing·ly
dev·as·ta·tion
dev·as·ta·tive
dev·as·ta·tor
de·vel·op
de·vel·op·able
de·vel·oped
de·vel·op·er
de·vel·op·ment
de·vel·op·men-
    tal·ly

de·vest
de·vi·ant
de·vi·ate
de·vi·at·ed
de·vi·a·tion
de·vi·a·tor
de·vice n. (invention)
de·vise v. (invent, will)
de·vised
de·vi·see
de·vi·sor
de·vo·lu·tion
de·vo·lu·tion·ary
de·vo·lu·tion·ist
de·volve
di·ag·no·ses pl.
di·ag·no·sis sing.
di·ag·nos·tic
di·ag·nos·ti·cian
di·ag·o·nal
di·ag·o·nal·ly
di·ar·i·um
di·as·to·le
di·a·stol·ic
dia·ther·mic
dia·ther·my
di·a·tribe
dic·ta or dic·tums
(sing.: *dictum*)
dic·tate
dic·tat·ed
dic·ta·tion
dic·ta·tor·ship
dic·tum (pl.: *dicta* or
dictums)
di·es non

dif·fer
dif·fered
dif·fer·ence
(variation; cf.
deference)
dif·fer·en·ti·ate
dif·fer·en·ti·a·tion
dif·fi·cult
dif·fi·cul·ty
dif·fuse
dif·fuse·ly
dif·fuse·ness
dif·fu·sion
dig·a·my
di·gest
di·gest·ed
di·gest·ibil·i·ty
di·gest·ible
di·ges·tion
di·ges·tive
dig·ni·fied
dig·ni·fy
dig·ni·ty
di·gress
di·gres·sion
di·ju·di·ca·tion
di·lap·i·dat·ed
di·lap·i·da·tion
di·la·ta·tion
dil·a·to·ry
di·lem·ma
dil·i·gence
dil·i·gent·ly
di·min·ish
di·min·ish·able
di·min·ish·ment

dim·i·nu·tio
dim·i·nu·tion
di·plo·ma·cy
dip·lo·ma·tic
dip·lo·mat·i·cal·ly
dip·so·ma·nia
dip·so·ma·ni·ac
dire
di·rect
di·rect·ed
di·rec·tion
di·rec·tive
di·rect·ly
di·rect·ness
di·rec·tor
di·rec·tor·ate
di·rec·to·ri·al
di·rec·to·ry
dire·ly
dire·ness
dis·abil·i·ties
dis·abil·i·ty
dis·able
dis·abled
dis·able·ment
dis·abling
dis·ac·cord
dis·ad·van·tage
dis·ad·van·ta·geous
dis·af·firm
dis·af·fir·mance
dis·af·fir·ma·tion
dis·agree·able
dis·agree·able·ness
dis·agree·ably
dis·agreed

dis·agree·ing
dis·agree·ment
dis·al·low
dis·al·low·ance
dis·al·lowed
dis·ap·pear
dis·ap·pear·ance
dis·ap·point·ment
dis·ap·prov·al
dis·ap·prove
dis·ap·proved
dis·ap·prov·ing·ly
dis·ar·range
dis·ar·ranged
di·sas·ter
di·sas·trous
di·sas·trous·ly
dis·avow
dis·avow·al
dis·avowed
dis·bar
dis·bar·ment
dis·barred
dis·bar·ring
dis·burse
dis·bursed
dis·burse·ment
dis·burs·er
dis·cern
dis·cerned
dis·cern·ible
dis·cern·ment
dis·charge
dis·charge·able
dis·charged
dis·charg·ee

dis·charg·er
dis·ci·pli·nar·i·an
dis·ci·plin·ary
dis·ci·pline
dis·ci·plined
dis·ci·plin·er
dis·claim
dis·claimed
dis·claim·er
dis·cla·ma·tion
dis·close
dis·closed
dis·clos·er
dis·clo·sure
dis·com·fort
dis·con·tin·u·ance
dis·con·tin·ue
dis·con·tin·ued
dis·con·tin·u·ing
dis·con·ti·nu·ity
dis·con·tin·u·ous
dis·cord
dis·cor·dant·ly
dis·count
dis·count·able
dis·count·ed
dis·count·er
dis·cour·age
dis·cour·aged
dis·cour·age·ment
dis·cour·ag·ing·ly
dis·cov·er
dis·cov·er·able
dis·cov·ered
dis·cov·er·er
dis·cov·er·ies

dis·cov·ert
dis·cov·er·ture
dis·cov·ery
dis·cred·it
dis·cred·it·able
dis·cred·it·ably
dis·cred·it·ed
dis·creet (prudent; cf. *discrete*)
dis·creet·ly
dis·creet·ness
dis·crep·an·cies
dis·crep·an·cy
dis·crep·ant
dis·crep·ant·ly
dis·crete (separate; cf. *discreet*)
dis·crete·ly
dis·crete·ness
dis·cre·tion
dis·cre·tion·ary
dis·crim·i·nate
dis·crim·i·nat·ed
dis·crim·i·nat·ing·ly
dis·crim·i·na·tion
dis·crim·i·na·tive·ly
dis·crim·i·na·tor
dis·crim·i·na·to·ry
dis·cuss
dis·cussed
dis·cuss·ing
dis·cus·sion
dis·ease (illness; cf. *disseise*)
dis·eased (sick; cf. *deceased*)

35

dis·fa·vor
dis·fig·ure
dis·fig·ured
dis·fig·ure·ment
dis·fran·chise
dis·fran·chise·ment
dis·grace
dis·grace·ful
dis·grace·ful·ly
dis·grace·ful·ness
dis·guise
dis·guised
dis·guis·ed·ly
dis·hon·est·ly
dis·hon·es·ty
dis·hon·or
dis·hon·or·able
dis·hon·ored
dis·hon·or·er
dis·il·lu·sion
dis·in·cli·na·tion
dis·in·clined
dis·in·her·it
dis·in·her·i·tance
dis·in·her·it·ed
dis·in·ter
dis·in·ter·est
dis·in·ter·est·ed
dis·in·ter·est·ed·ly
dis·in·ter·est·ed-
   ness
dis·in·ter·ment
dis·in·terred
dis·in·ter·ring
dis·junct
dis·junc·tion

dis·junc·tive·ly
dis·lo·cate
dis·lo·cat·ed
dis·lo·ca·tion
dis·loy·al
dis·loy·al·ly
dis·loy·al·ty
dis·miss
dis·miss·al
dis·missed
dis·obe·di·ence
dis·obey
dis·obeyed
dis·obey·ing
dis·or·der
dis·or·dered
dis·or·der·li·ness
dis·or·der·ly
dis·par·age
dis·par·age·ment
dis·par·ag·ing·ly
dis·pa·rate (different;
   cf. *desperate*)
dis·pas·sion·ate·ly
dis·patch
dis·patched
dis·patch·er
dis·pel
dis·pelled
dis·pel·ling
dis·pens·abil·i·ty
dis·pens·able
dis·pen·sa·ry
dis·pen·sa·tion
dis·pense
dis·pensed

dis·pens·er
dis·place
dis·place·able
dis·placed
dis·place·ment
dis·play
dis·played
dis·pos·able
dis·pos·al
dis·pose
dis·posed
dis·pos·ing
dis·po·si·tion
dis·pos·sess
dis·pos·sessed
dis·pos·sess·ing
dis·pos·ses·sion
dis·pos·ses·sor
dis·proof
dis·prov·able
dis·prove
dis·proved
dis·put·abil·i·ty
dis·put·able
dis·pu·tant
dis·pu·ta·tion
dis·pute
dis·put·ed
dis·qual·i·fi·ca·tion
dis·qual·i·fied
dis·qual·i·fy
dis·qual·i·fy·ing
dis·re·gard
dis·re·gard·ed
dis·re·pair
dis·rep·u·ta·ble

dis·rep·u·ta·ble·ness
dis·rep·u·ta·bly
dis·re·pute
dis·re·spect
dis·rupt
dis·rupt·ed
dis·rup·tion
dis·rup·tive
dis·sat·is·fac·tion
dis·sat·is·fac·to·ry
dis·sect
dis·sect·ed
dis·sec·tion
dis·seise   or
  dis·seize
  (dispossess; cf.
  disease)
dis·sei·sin   or
  dis·sei·zin
dis·seis·i·tus
dis·seis·or   or
  dis·sei·zor
dis·seis·or·ess
dis·sem·ble
  (disguise)
dis·sem·bler
dis·sem·bling
dis·sen·sion
dis·sent
  (disagreement; cf.
  decent, descent)
dis·sent·ed
dis·sent·er
dis·si·pate
dis·si·pat·ed
dis·si·pa·tion

dis·so·ci·a·tion
dis·sol·u·bil·i·ty
dis·sol·u·ble
dis·so·lute
dis·so·lute·ly
dis·so·lute·ness
dis·so·lu·tion
dis·sol·u·tive
dis·solv·able
dis·solve
dis·solved
dis·suade
dis·suad·ed
dis·suad·er
dis·sua·sive
dis·tal
dis·tance
dis·ten·sion   or
  dis·ten·tion
dis·till
dis·tilled
dis·till·ery
dis·tinct
dis·tinc·tion
dis·tinc·tive·ly
dis·tinct·ly
dis·tinct·ness
dis·tin·guish
dis·tin·guish·able
dis·tin·guish·ably
dis·tin·guished
dis·tort
dis·tort·ed
dis·tor·tion
dis·tra·here
dis·train

dis·train·er   or
  dis·trai·nor
dis·traint
dis·traught
dis·traught·ly
dis·tress
dis·tressed
dis·tress·ing
dis·trib·ut·able
dis·trib·ute
dis·trib·ut·ed
dis·trib·u·tee
dis·tri·bu·tion
dis·tri·bu·tion·al
dis·trib·u·tive
dis·trib·u·tive·ly
dis·trib·u·tor
dis·trict
di·strin·gas
dis·trust·ful
dis·turb
dis·tur·bance
dis·turbed
dis·turb·er
di·verge
di·ver·gence
di·ver·gent·ly
di·vers   (various)
di·verse   (different)
di·verse·ly
di·verse·ness
di·ver·si·fi·ca·tion
di·ver·si·fied
di·ver·si·fy
di·ver·sion
di·ver·sion·ary

di·ver·sion·ist
di·ver·si·ty
di·vest·ed
di·ves·ti·ture
di·vest·ment
di·vide
di·vid·ed
div·i·dend
di·vis·i·bil·i·ty
di·vis·i·ble
di·vis·i·bly
di·vi·sion·al
di·vi·sive
di·vi·sive·ly
di·vi·sive·ness
di·vorce
di·vorced
di·vor·cée
di·vorce·ment
di·vulge
di·vulged
di·vul·gence
diz·zi·ness
diz·zy
dock·et
dock·et·ed
doc·tor
doc·tri·nal
doc·trine
doc·u·ment
doc·u·ment·able
doc·u·men·tal
doc·u·men·tar·i·an
doc·u·men·tar·i·ly
doc·u·men·ta·ry
doc·u·men·ta·tion

doc·u·ment·ed
dog·ma
dog·mat·ic
dog·mat·i·cal·ly
dol·lar
do·main
do·mes·tic
do·mes·ti·cal·ly
do·mes·ti·cate
do·mes·ti·ca·tion
do·mi·cile
do·mi·ciled
do·mi·cil·i·ary
dom·i·nant
dom·i·nate
dom·i·nat·ed
dom·i·na·tion
dom·i·na·tive
dom·i·na·tor
dom·i·neer·ing
do·min·ion
do·nate
do·nat·ed
do·na·tio in·ter
  vi·vos
do·na·tio mor·tis
  cau·sa
do·na·tion
do·na·tive
do·na·tor
do·nee
do·nor
doped
dop·ing
dor·man·cy
dor·mant

dor·mi·ent
dor·sal
dor·si·flex·ion
dos·age
dos·sier
dot·age
do·tal
dot·ard
do·ta·tion
dou·ble
dou·bled
dou·bling
dou·bly
doubt·ed
doubt·ful·ly
dove·tail
dow·able
dow·a·ger
dow·er
dow·ry
dra·co·ni·an
draft·ed
drafts·man·ship
dragged
drag·ging
drain·age
draw·back n.
draw·ee
draw·er
drawn
dray·age
dredge
dredged
dredg·er
dredg·ing
drink·able

38

drink·er
droit
droi·tu·ral
drugged
drug·ging
drug·gist
drunk·ard
drunk·en
drunk·en·ness
drunk·o·me·ter
du·al (twofold; cf.
    duel)
du·al·ism
du·al·i·ty
du·al·ly
du·bi·ous
du·bi·ous·ly
du·bi·ous·ness
du·bi·ta·ble
du·ces te·cum
due·bill
du·el (combat; cf.
    dual)
du·ly
dumb—bid·ding
dum be·ne se
    ges·se·rit
dumb·found
dum·my
dun·geon
dun·nage
dunned
dun·ning
du·plex
du·pli·cate
du·pli·cat·ed

du·pli·ca·tion
du·pli·ca·tive
du·pli·ca·tor
du·plic·i·ties
du·plic·i·ty
du·ra·bil·i·ty
du·ra·ble·ness
du·ra·bly
du·ran·te
    ab·sen·tia
du·ran·te fu·ro·re
du·ran·te
    mi·no·re
    ae·ta·te
du·ran·te
    vi·du·i·ta·te
du·ran·te vi·ta
du·ra·tion
du·ress
du·res·sor
du·ti·able
du·ties
du·ti·ful
du·ti·ful·ly
du·ty
dwelled
dwell·er
dwell·ing
dys·func·tion
dys·no·my
dys·pa·reu·nia
dys·pha·gia
dys·pha·sia
dys·pnea
dys·tro·phy
dys·uria

E

ear·mark
ear·marked
earn·er
ear·nest·ly
ear·nest·ness
ear—wit·ness
ease·ment
eaves·drop
eaves·dropped
eaves·drop·per
eaves·drop·ping
ebri·e·ty
ec·cen·tric
ec·cen·tri·cal·ly
ec·cen·tric·i·ty
ec·chy·mo·ses pl.
ec·chy·mo·sis sing.
ec·cle·si·as·tic
ec·cle·si·as·ti·cal·ly
eclec·tic
eco·nom·ic
eco·nom·i·cal·ly
econ·o·mies
econ·o·mize
econ·o·my
e con·ver·so
ec·u·men·i·cal
ede·ma
edict
edic·tal

edi·tion (printing; cf. *addition*)
ed·u·cate
ed·u·cat·ed
ed·u·ca·tion·al·ly
ed·u·ca·tive
ed·u·ca·tor
ef·fect (result; cf. *affect*)
ef·fect·ed
ef·fect·er
ef·fec·tive·ly
ef·fec·tive·ness
ef·fec·tu·al
ef·fec·tu·al·i·ty
ef·fec·tu·al·ly
ef·fec·tu·al·ness
ef·fec·tu·ate
ef·fec·tu·at·ed
ef·fi·cien·cy
ef·fi·cient·ly
ef·fi·gy
ef·flu·ence
ef·flu·ent
ef·flux
ef·flux·ion
ef·fort
ef·frac·tion
ef·frac·tor
egress
egres·sion
eject
eject·able
eject·ed
ejec·tion
ejec·tive

eject·ment
ejec·tor
ejur·a·tion
elas·tic
elas·tic·i·ty
el·der
el·dest
elec·tion
elec·tion·eer
elec·tive·ly
elec·tor
elec·tor·al
elec·tor·ate
elec·tric
elec·tri·cal·ly
elec·tric·i·ty
elec·tro·car·dio·gram
elec·tro·car·dio·graph
elec·tro·car·di·og·ra·phy
elec·tro·cute
elec·tro·cut·ed
elec·tro·cu·tion
elec·tro·en·ceph·a·lo·gram
elec·tro·en·ceph·a·lo·graph
el·ee·mos·y·nary
el·e·ment
el·e·men·tal·ly
el·e·men·ta·ry
el·e·va·tor
elic·it (evoke; cf. *illicit*)

elic·i·ta·tion
elic·it·ed
elic·i·tor
el·i·gi·bil·i·ty
el·i·gi·ble (qualified; cf. *illegible*)
el·i·gi·bly
elim·i·nate
elim·i·nat·ed
elim·i·na·tion
elim·i·na·tive
elim·i·na·to·ry
el·lip·ses pl.
el·lip·sis sing.
eloign
eloign·ment
elope
eloped
elope·ment
elop·er
else·where
elu·ci·date
elu·ci·da·tion
elude (escape; cf. *allude*)
elud·ed
elu·sion (escape; cf. *allusion, illusion*)
elu·sive
em·a·nate
em·a·nat·ed
em·a·na·tion
em·a·na·tion·al
em·a·na·tive
eman·ci·pate
eman·ci·pat·ed

eman·ci·pa·tion·ist
eman·ci·pa·tor
eman·ci·pa·to·ry
em·bar·go
em·bar·goes
em·bark
em·bar·ka·tion
em·barked
em·bar·rass
em·bar·rassed
em·bar·rass·es
em·bar·rass·ing·ly
em·bar·rass·ment
em·bas·sy
em·bez·zle
em·bez·zled
em·bez·zle·ment
em·bez·zler
em·bez·zling
em·ble·ments
em·bo·lism
em·bo·lus
em·brace·able
em·braced
em·brace·ment
em·brac·er
em·brac·ery
emerge
emerged
emer·gence
emer·gen·cies
emer·gen·cy
emer·gent
em·i·grant (one de-
parting; cf. *immi-*
grant)

em·i·grate (depart;
cf. *immigrate*)
em·i·grat·ed
em·i·gra·tion
em·i·nence
(prominence; cf.
imminence)
em·i·nent
(prominent; cf.
imminent)
em·i·nent·ly
em·is·sary
emis·sion
emis·sive
emis·siv·i·ty
emit·ted
emit·ter
emit·ting
emol·u·ment
em·pan·el
em·pan·eled
em·pan·el·ing
em·pha·ses pl.
em·pha·sis sing.
em·pha·size
em·pha·sized
em·phat·ic
em·phat·i·cal·ly
em·phy·se·ma
em·phy·se·ma·tous
em·pir·ic
em·pir·i·cal
em·pir·i·cal·ly
em·pir·i·cism
em·pir·i·cist
em·plead

em·ploy·abil·i·ty
em·ploy·able
em·ployed
em·ploy·ee *or*
em·ploye
em·ploy·er
em·ploy·ment
em·pow·er
em·pow·ered
em·pow·er·ment
em·py·ema
en·able
en·abled
en·abling
en·act·ed
en·act·ment
en·ac·tor
en·ceinte
en·close
en·closed
en·clo·sure
en·coun·ter
en·coun·tered
en·cour·age
en·cour·aged
en·cour·age·ment
en·cour·ag·ing·ly
en·croach
en·croached
en·croach·ment
en·cum·ber
en·cum·bered
en·cum·brance
en·cum·branc·er
en·cum·branc·es
en·dan·ger

en·dan·gered
en·dan·ger·ment
en·deav·or
en·deav·ored
en·dors·able
en·dorse
en·dorsed
en·dors·ee
en·dorse·ment
en·dors·er
en·dow
en·dowed
en·dow·ment
en·dur·ance
en·dure
en·dured
en·dur·ing·ly
en·e·mies
en·e·my
en·feoff
en·feoff·ment
en·force
en·force·abil·i·ty
en·force·able
en·forced
en·force·ment
en·forc·er
en·fran·chise
en·fran·chised
en·fran·chise·ment
en·gage
en·gaged
en·gage·ment
en·gag·ing·ly
en·gen·der
en·gen·dered

en·gine
en·gi·neer
en·hance
en·hanced
en·hance·ment
en·join
en·joined
en·joy·ment
en·large
en·large·able
en·larged
en·large·ment
en·larg·er
en·list·ed
en·list·ment
enor·mi·ty
enor·mous·ly
enor·mous·ness
en·rich
en·riched
en·rich·er
en·rich·ment
en·roll *or* en·rol
en·rolled
en·roll·ee
en·roll·ing
en·roll·ment *or*
    en·rol·ment
en·seal
ens le·gis
en·sue
en·su·ing
en·tail
en·tailed
en·tail·er
en·tail·ment

en·ter
en·tered
en·ter·i·tis
en·ter·prise
en·ter·tain
en·ter·tained
en·ter·tain·er
en·ter·tain·ment
en·thu·si·ast
en·thu·si·as·tic
en·thu·si·as·ti·cal·ly
en·tice
en·ticed
en·tice·ment
en·tic·ing·ly
en·tire·ly
en·tire·ness
en·tire·ty
en·ti·tle
en·ti·tled
en·ti·tle·ment
en·ti·tling
en·ti·ty
en·trance
en·tranced
en·trance·ment
en·tranc·ing·ly
en·trap
en·trap·ment
en·treat
en·treat·ing·ly
en·treat·ment
en·treaty
en·tre·pôt
en·tries
en·try

enu·mer·ate
enu·mer·at·ed
enu·mer·a·tion
enu·mer·a·tive
enu·mer·a·tor
en·ure
en·vel·op
   v. (enclose)
en·vel·ope
   n. (mailing)
en·vel·oped
en·vel·op·ment
en·voy
eo in·stan·ti
eo ip·so
eo nom·i·ne
ep·i·dem·ic
ep·i·dem·i·cal·ly
ep·i·lep·sy
ep·i·lep·tic
e plu·ri·bus
  unum
ep·och
ep·och·al
ep·och·al·ly
equal
equaled *or*
  equalled
equal·ing *or*
  equal·ling
equal·i·ty
equal·iza·tion
equal·ize
equal·ized
equal·iz·er
equal·ly

equip·ment
equipped
equip·ping
eq·ui·ta·ble
eq·ui·ta·ble·ness
eq·ui·ta·bly
eq·ui·ties
eq·ui·ty
equiv·a·lence
equiv·a·len·cy
equiv·a·lent
equiv·o·cal
equiv·o·cal·i·ty
equiv·o·cal·ly
equiv·o·cal·ness
equiv·o·cate
equiv·o·cat·ed
equiv·o·ca·tion
equiv·o·ca·tor
erect (build; cf. *arrect*)
erect·ed
erec·tion
erect·ly
erect·ness
erec·tor
ero·sion·al
ero·sive·ness
ero·siv·i·ty
err
er·rant
er·rant·ly
er·ra·ta (sing.:
  erratum)
er·rat·ic
er·rat·i·cal·ly
er·ra·tum (pl.: *errata*)

erred
err·ing
er·ro·ne·ous·ly
er·ro·ne·ous·ness
er·ror
es·ca·late
es·ca·lat·ed
es·ca·la·tion
es·ca·la·tor
es·cape
es·caped
es·cap·ee
es·cap·er
es·cheat
es·cheat·able
es·crow
es·ne·cy
es·pous·al
es·pouse
es·poused
es·pous·er
es·quire
es·se
es·sence
es·sen·tial
es·sen·ti·al·i·ty
es·sen·tial·ly
es·sen·tial·ness
es·tab·lish
es·tab·lished
es·tab·lish·er
es·tab·lish·ment
es·tate
es·ti·mate
es·ti·mat·ed
es·ti·ma·tion

es·ti·ma·tive
es·ti·ma·tor
es·top
es·topped
es·top·pel
es·top·ping
es·to·vers
es·tray
es·treat
es·trepe
es·trepe·ment
es·tu·ary
et al. (abbreviation of *et alii, et alius*)
et alii (and others)
et alios (and other things)
et alius (and others)
et als. (abbreviation of *et alios*)
etc. (abbreviation of *et cetera*)
et cet·era (and so forth)
et·cet·era (odds and ends)
eth·i·cal
eth·i·cal·i·ty
eth·i·cal·ly
eth·i·cal·ness
eth·ics
et non
et seq. (abbreviation of *et sequens, et sequentes, et sequitur*)

et se·quens (and the following one)
et se·quen·tes (and those that follow)
et se·qui·tur (and as follows)
et sic
et ux. (abbreviation of *et uxor*)
et ux·or
et vir
evade
evad·ed
evad·er
eval·u·ate
eval·u·at·ed
eval·u·a·tion
eval·u·a·tive
eva·sion
eva·sive·ly
eva·sive·ness
event·ful·ly
event·ful·ness
even·tu·al
even·tu·al·i·ty
even·tu·al·ly
even·tu·ate
ev·ery
evict·ed
evic·tion
evic·tor
ev·i·dence
ev·i·denced
ev·i·dent
ev·i·den·tial

ev·i·den·tial·ly
ev·i·den·tia·ry
ev·i·dent·ly
evo·lu·tion
evo·lu·tion·ary
evo·lu·tion·ism
evo·lu·tion·ist
evolve
evolved
evolve·ment
ex·ac·er·bate
ex·ac·er·bat·ed
ex·ac·er·ba·tion
ex·act
ex·act·ed
ex·ac·tion
ex·ac·ti·tude
ex·act·ly
ex·act·ness
ex·am·i·na·tion
ex·am·ine
ex·am·ined
ex·am·in·er
ex ca·the·dra
ex·ceed (surpass; cf. *accede*)
ex·cept (exclude; cf. *accept*)
ex·cept·ed
ex·cep·tion
ex·cep·tion·able
ex·cep·tion·al
ex·cep·tion·al·i·ty
ex·cep·tion·al·ly
ex·cerpt
ex·cerpt·ed

44

ex·cerpt·ing
ex·cerp·tion
ex·cess (surplus; cf. *access*)
ex·ces·sive
ex·ces·sive·ly
ex·ces·sive·ness
ex·change
ex·change·able
ex·changed
ex·chang·er
ex·cis·able
ex·cise
ex·cised
ex·ci·sion
ex·cit·abil·i·ty
ex·cit·able
ex·cite
ex·cit·ed
ex·cite·ment
ex·clud·abil·i·ty
ex·clud·able *or* ex·clud·ible
ex·clude
ex·clud·ed
ex·clud·er
ex·clu·sion
ex·clu·sion·ary
ex·clu·sion·ist
ex·clu·sive·ly
ex·clu·sive·ness
ex con·trac·tu
ex·cul·pate
ex·cul·pa·tion
ex·cul·pa·to·ry
ex cu·ria

ex·cus·able
ex·cus·ably
ex·cu·sa·to·ry
ex·cuse
ex·cused
ex·cus·er
ex·cuss
ex de·bi·to jus·ti·ti·ae
ex de·lic·to
ex di·rec·to
ex·e·cute
ex·e·cut·ed
ex·e·cu·tion
ex·e·cu·tion·er
ex·ec·u·tive
ex·ec·u·tor mas.
ex·ec·u·to·ri·al
ex·ec·u·to·ry
ex·ec·u·trix fem.
ex·em·pla·ry
ex·em·pli·fi·ca·tion
ex·em·pli·fy
ex·empt·ed
ex·empt·ible
ex·emp·tion
ex·er·cise
ex·er·cised
ex·er·cis·er
ex gra·tia
ex·haust·ed
ex·haus·tive
ex·hib·it
ex·hib·it·ed
ex·hi·bi·tion
ex·hi·bi·tion·er

ex·hi·bi·tion·ist
ex·hib·i·tor
ex·hort
ex·hor·ta·tion
ex·hort·ed
ex·hu·ma·tion
ex·hume
ex·humed
ex·hum·er
ex·i·gence
ex·i·gen·cies
ex·i·gen·cy
ex·i·gent·ly
ex·i·gi·ble
ex·ile
ex·ist·ed
ex·is·tence
ex·is·tent
ex·i·tus
ex jus·ta cau·sa
ex le·ge
ex ma·le·fi·cio
ex mero motu
ex ne·ces·si·ta·te le·gis
ex of·fi·cio
ex·on·er·ate
ex·on·er·at·ed
ex·on·er·at·ing
ex·on·er·a·tion
ex·on·er·a·tive
ex·or·bi·tance
ex·or·bi·tant
ex par·te
ex·pa·tri·ate
ex·pa·tri·a·tion

ex·pect·able
ex·pec·tance
ex·pec·tan·cy
ex·pec·tant
ex·pec·tant·ly
ex·pec·ta·tion
ex·pect·ed
ex·pe·di·ence
ex·pe·di·en·cy
ex·pe·di·ent
ex·pe·di·en·tial
ex·pe·di·ent·ly
ex·pe·di·ment
ex·pe·dite
ex·pe·dit·ed
ex·pe·dit·er
ex·pe·di·tion
ex·pe·di·tious·ly
ex·pe·di·tious·ness
ex·pel
ex·pelled
ex·pel·ling
ex·pend
ex·pend·abil·i·ty
ex·pend·able
ex·pend·ed
ex·pend·er
ex·pen·di·tor
ex·pen·di·ture
ex·pense
ex·pens·es
ex·pen·sive
ex·pe·ri·ence
ex·per·i·ment
ex·per·i·men·tal·ly
ex·per·i·men·ta·tion

ex·per·i·ment·ed
ex·per·i·ment·er
ex·pert
ex·per·tise n.
ex·pert·ism
ex·pert·ize v.
ex·pert·ly
ex·pert·ness
ex·pi·ate
ex·pi·at·ed
ex·pi·a·tion
ex·pi·ra·tion
ex·pir·ato·ry
ex·pire
ex·pired
ex·plain
ex·plained
ex·pla·na·tion
ex·plan·a·to·ry
ex·pli·ca·ble
ex·pli·cate
ex·pli·ca·tion
ex·pli·ca·tive
ex·pli·ca·tor
ex·plic·it
ex·plic·it·ly
ex·plic·it·ness
ex·ploit·able
ex·ploi·ta·tion
ex·ploit·ative
ex·ploit·ative·ly
ex·ploit·ed
ex·ploit·er
ex·plo·ra·tion
ex·plor·ative
ex·plor·ato·ry

ex·plo·sion
ex·plo·sive
ex·plo·sive·ly
ex·plo·sive·ness
ex·port·able
ex·por·ta·tion
ex·port·ed
ex·port·er
ex·pose v.
ex·po·sé n.
ex·posed
ex·pos·er
ex·pos·it
ex·po·si·tion
ex·po·si·tion·al
ex·pos·i·tive
ex·pos·i·tor
ex·pos·i·to·ry
ex post fac·to
ex·po·sure
ex·press
ex·pressed
ex·press·ible
ex·pres·sion·less
ex·pres·sive·ly
ex·pres·sive·ness
ex·press·ly
ex·pro·mis·sor
ex·pro·pri·ate
ex·pro·pri·at·ed
ex·pro·pri·a·tion
ex·pro·pri·a·tor
ex pro·prio
     mo·tu
ex pro·prio
     vi·go·re

ex·pulse
ex·pulsed
ex·pul·sion
ex·pul·sive
ex·punc·tion
ex·punge
ex·punged
ex·pung·er
ex·pur·gate
ex·pur·gat·ed
ex·pur·ga·tion
ex·pur·ga·tor
ex·pur·ga·to·ri·al
ex·pur·ga·to·ry
ex·purge
ex sta·tu·to
ex·tant (existing; cf. *extent*)
ex·tend·ed
ex·tend·ible
ex·ten·sion
ex·ten·sion·al
ex·ten·sion·al·ly
ex·ten·sive·ly
ex·tent (degree; cf. *extant*)
ex·ten·u·ate
ex·ten·u·at·ed
ex·ten·u·at·ing
ex·ten·u·a·tion
ex·ten·u·a·tor
ex·ten·u·a·to·ry
ex·te·ri·or
ex·te·ri·or·ly
ex·te·ri·or·ize
ex·ter·mi·nate

ex·ter·mi·nat·ed
ex·ter·mi·nat·ing
ex·ter·mi·na·tion
ex·ter·nal
ex·ter·nal·iza·tion
ex·ter·nal·ize
ex·ter·nal·ly
ex·ter·ri·to·ri·al
ex·ter·ri·to·ri·al·i·ty
ex·tinct
ex·tinc·tion
ex·tinc·tive
ex·tin·guish·able
ex·tin·guished
ex·tin·guish·er
ex·tin·guish·ment
ex·tor·sive·ly
ex·tort·ed
ex·tort·er
ex·tort·ing
ex·tor·tion
ex·tor·tion·ary
ex·tor·tion·ate
ex·tor·tion·er
ex·tor·tion·ist
ex·tor·tive
ex·tract
ex·tract·able *or* ex·tract·ible
ex·tract·ed
ex·trac·tion
ex·trac·tive
ex·tra·dit·able
ex·tra·dite
ex·tra·dit·ed
ex·tra·dit·ing

ex·tra·di·tion
ex·tra·do·tal
ex·tra·haz·ard·ous
ex·tra·ju·di·cial
ex·tra·ju·di·cial·ly
ex·tra·le·gal
ex·tra·mar·i·tal
ex·tra·mar·i·tal·ly
ex·tra·ne·ous
ex·tra·ne·ous·ly
ex·tra·ne·ous·ness
ex·traor·di·nar·i·ly
ex·traor·di·nary
ex·tra·ter·ri·to·ri·al
ex·tra·ter·ri·to·ri·al·i·ty
ex·trav·a·gance
ex·trav·a·gant·ly
ex·trav·a·sa·tion
ex·treme·ly
ex·tre·mis
ex·trem·ism
ex·trem·ist
ex·trem·i·ty
ex·tri·ca·ble
ex·tri·cate
ex·tri·cat·ed
ex·tri·cat·ing
ex·tri·ca·tion
ex·trin·sic
ex·trin·si·cal·ly
ex·tro·ver·sion
ex·tro·vert
ex·u·date
ex·u·da·tion
eye·wit·ness

47

F

fab·ri·cate
fab·ri·cat·ed
fab·ri·ca·tion
fab·ri·ca·tor
fa·ci·as
fac·ile
fac·ile·ly
fac·ile·ness
fa·cil·i·tate
fa·cil·i·tat·ed
fa·cil·i·ta·tion
fa·cil·i·ties
fa·cil·i·ty
fac·ing
fac·sim·i·le
fac·tion
fac·to
fac·tor
fac·tor·able
fac·tor·age
fac·tor·ship
fac·to·ry
fac·tu·al
fac·tu·al·ism
fac·tu·al·ist
fac·tu·al·i·ty
fac·tu·al·ly
fac·tu·al·ness
fac·tum
fac·ul·ta·tive

fac·ul·ta·tive·ly
fac·ul·ties
fac·ul·ty
failed
fail·ure
fair·ly
fair·ness
fait ac·com·pli sing.
faith·ful
faith·ful·ly
faith·ful·ness
faith·less·ly
faith·less·ness
faits ac·com·plis pl.
fal·low
false·hood
false·ly
false·ness
fal·si·fi·ca·tion
fal·si·fied
fal·si·fi·er
fal·si·fy
fal·si·fy·ing
fal·si·ty
fa·mil·iar
fa·mil·iar·i·ty
fa·mil·iar·iza·tion
fa·mil·iar·ize
fa·mil·iar·ly
fam·i·ly
fa·nat·ic
fa·nat·i·cal·ly
fa·nat·i·cism
fa·nat·i·cize

fan·ci·ful·ly
fas·cism
fas·cist
fas·cis·tic
fa·tal
fa·tal·ism
fa·tal·ist
fa·tal·is·tic
fa·tal·is·ti·cal·ly
fa·tal·i·ty
fa·tal·ly
fath·om
fault·i·ly
fault·i·ness
fault·less·ly
fault·less·ness
faux pas sing., pl.
fa·vor·able
fa·vor·ably
fa·vored
fa·vor·ite
fa·vor·it·ism
fe·al
fe·al·ty
fea·sance
fea·si·bil·i·ty
fea·si·ble
fea·si·ble·ness
fea·si·bly
feas·or
fed·er·al
fed·er·al·ly
fed·er·a·tion
fee·ble·mind·ed·
    ness
fee·ble·ness

48

fee·bler
fee·blest
fee·bly
feign
feigned
feign·er
feign·ing
felo—de—se
fel·on
fe·lo·ni·ous
fe·lo·ni·ous·ly
fe·lo·ni·ous·ness
fel·on·ry
fel·o·ny
fe·male
feme cov·ert
feme sole
fem·i·cide
fem·i·nine·ly
fem·i·nine·ness
fem·i·nin·i·ty
fem·i·nism
fem·i·nist
fe·mur
fen·er·a·tion
feoff·ee
feoff·ment
feof·for
fe·rae na·tu·rae
fe·tal
fe·ti·cide
fet·ter
fet·tered
fe·tus
fi·at
fi·bril·la·tion

fib·u·la
fic·tion·al·iza·tion
fic·tion·al·ize
fic·tion·al·ly
fic·ti·tious·ly
fic·ti·tious·ness
fi·dei·com·mis·sum
fi·del·i·ty
fi·des
fi·du·cial
fi·du·cial·ly
fi·du·ciary
fief
fi·eri fa·ci·as
   (abbrev.: *fi. fa.*)
fig·u·ra·tive·ly
fil·ial
fil·i·a·tion
fil·i·bus·ter
fil·i·bus·tered
fi·li·us nul·li·us
fi·li·us po·pu·li
filth·i·ly
filth·i·ness
filthy
fi·na·gle
fi·na·gled
fi·na·gling
fi·nal·i·ty
fi·nal·iza·tion
fi·nal·ize
fi·nal·ly
fi·nance
fi·nanced
fi·nanc·es
fi·nan·cial·ly

fi·nan·cier
find·er
fin·ger
fin·gered
fin·ger·print n., v.
fin·ger·print·ed
fi·nis
fi·nite
fire·arm
fire·man
fire·works
firm·ly
firm·ness
first class n.
first—class adj.,
   adv.
fis·cal (financial; cf.
   physical)
fis·cal·ly
fix·a·tion
fix·ture
flac·cid
fla·grant
fla·gran·te
   de·lic·to
fla·grant·ly
flat·tered
flat·ter·er
flat·ter·ing·ly
flat·tery
float·able
float·ed
float·er
flog
flogged
flog·ging

49

flot·sam
flume
flu·o·ro·scope
flu·o·ro·scop·ic
flu·o·ros·co·py
fly—pow·er
fo·lio
fo·ment
fo·men·ta·tion
fo·ment·er
foot·print
for·bear·ance
force·ful·ly
force·ful·ness
force·less
forc·i·ble
forc·i·ble·ness
forc·i·bly
fore·bear *or*
    for·bear
fore·cast·ed
fore·cast·er
fore·close
fore·closed
fore·clo·sure
fore·go
for·eign
for·eign·er
fore·man·ship
fore·noon
fo·ren·sic
fo·ren·si·cal·ly
fore·see
fore·see·abil·i·ty
fore·see·able
fore·sight

fore·sight·ed
fore·sight·ed·ness
fore·stall
fore·warned
for·feit
for·feit·able
for·feit·ed
for·feit·er
for·fei·ture
forge
forged
forg·er
forg·ery
forg·ing
for·mal
for·mal·i·ty
for·mal·ize
for·mal·ly
    (ceremonially)
form·er·ly
    (previously)
for·mu·la sing.
for·mu·las pl.
for·mu·late
for·mu·lat·ed
for·mu·la·tion
for·mu·la·tor
for·mu·li·za·tion
for·mu·lize
for·ni·cate
for·ni·cat·ed
for·ni·ca·tion
for·swear *or*
    fore·swear
for·sworn *or*
    fore·sworn

forth·com·ing
forth·right
forth·with
for·ti·tude
for·tu·itous·ly
for·tu·itous·ness
for·tu·ity
for·tu·nate·ly
for·tune
fo·rum
for·ward·ed
for·ward·ly
for·ward·ness
fos·ter
fos·ter·age
fos·tered
fos·ter·er
fos·ter·ling
foun·da·tion
foun·da·tion·al
found·ed
found·er
found·ling
frac·tion·al
frac·tion·al·ize
frac·tion·al·ly
frac·tion·ation
frac·tion·ator
frac·ture
frac·tured
fran·chise
fran·chised
franked
fra·ter·nal
fra·ter·nal·ism
fra·ter·nal·ly

fra·ter·ni·ty
frat·er·ni·za·tion
frat·er·nize
frat·er·nized
frat·er·niz·er
frat·ri·cide
fraud
fraud·u·lence
fraud·u·lent·ly
free·dom
free·hold
free·hold·er
freight·age
freight·er
fre·quen·cy
fre·quent
fre·quen·ta·tion
fre·quent·ed
fre·quent·er
fre·quent·ly
fre·quent·ness
fric·tion
fright·en
fright·ened
fri·vol·i·ty
friv·o·lous·ly
friv·o·lous·ness
front·age
fron·tal
front·ed
fron·tier
fro·zen
fruc·tus
frus·trate
frus·trat·ed
frus·tra·tion

fu·gi·tive
fu·gi·tive·ly
ful·fill   *or*   ful·fil
ful·filled
ful·fill·er
ful·fill·ing
ful·fill·ment
full·blood·ed
full·ness
ful·ly
func·tion·al
func·tion·al·ism
func·tion·al·is·tic
func·tion·al·ly
func·tion·ary
func·tioned
func·tion·less
fun·da·men·tal·ist
fun·da·men·tal·ly
fund·ed
fu·ner·al
fun·gi·bil·i·ty
fun·gi·ble
fur·lough
fur·loughed
fur·nished
fur·ni·ture
fur·ther
fur·ther·ance
fur·thered
fur·ther·more
fur·ther·most
fur·thest
fur·tive
fur·tive·ly
fur·tive·ness

fu·sil·lade
fu·tile
fu·tile·ly
fu·tile·ness
fu·til·i·ty
fu·ture

gain·ful
gain·ful·ly
gain·ful·ness
gal·ley   proof
gal·lon
gal·lows
gam·ble
gam·bled
gam·bler
gam·bling
gang·land
gan·grene
gan·gre·nous
gang·ster
gang·ster·ism
gar·nish
gar·nish·ee
gar·nish·eed
gar·nish·ee·ing
gar·nish·er
gar·nish·ment

gar·rote *or*
  ga·rotte
gar·rot·ed *or*
  gar·rot·ted
gar·rot·er
gar·rot·ing *or*
  gar·rot·ting
gas·eous·ness
gas·o·line *or*
  gas·o·lene
gassed
gas·sing
gath·er
gath·ered
gath·er·er
gav·el
gav·eled *or*
  gav·elled
gav·el·ing *or*
  gav·el·ling
ge·ne·a·log·i·cal·ly
ge·ne·al·o·gist
ge·ne·al·o·gy
gen·era (sing.: *genus*)
gen·er·al
gen·er·al·i·ty
gen·er·al·iza·tion
gen·er·al·ize
gen·er·al·ized
gen·er·al·ly
gen·er·a·tion
ge·ner·ic
gen·er·os·i·ty
gen·er·ous·ly
gen·i·tal
gen·i·ta·lia

geno·ci·dal
geno·cide
gen·u·ine·ly
ge·nus (pl.: *genera*)
ger·i·at·rics
ger·mane·ly
ges·ta·tion
ges·ta·tion·al
ghast·ly
gift·ed
gist
give—and—take n.
giv·er
good·will
gov·ern·able
gov·erned
gov·ern·ment
gov·ern·men·tal
gov·ern·men·tal·ize
gov·ern·men·tal·ly
gov·er·nor
grad·u·al·ly
grad·u·ate
grad·u·at·ed
grad·u·a·tion
gra·dus
graft·er
grand·child
grand·chil·dren
grand·daugh·ter
grand·fa·ther
grand·moth·er
grand·son
grant·able
grant·ed
grant·ee

grant·or
graph·ic
graph·i·cal·ly
graph·ic·ness
grap·ple
grap·pled
grap·pling
grat·i·fi·ca·tion
grat·i·fied
grat·i·fy·ing
gra·tis
grat·i·tude
gra·tu·itous·ly
gra·tu·itous·ness
gra·tu·ity
gra·va·men sing.
gra·va·mens *or*
  gra·va·mi·na pl.
gra·vis
green·back
gre·nade
griev·ance
grieve
grieved
griev·ous·ly
griev·ous·ness
gross·ly
gross·ness
gru·el·ing *or*
  gru·el·ling
grue·some·ly
grue·some·ness
guar·an·tee v., n.
guar·an·teed
guar·an·tee·ing
guar·an·tor

guar·an·ty n.
guard·ian
guard·ian·ship
guer·ril·la *or*
  gue·ril·la
guid·ance
guid·ed
guile
guile·ful
guile·ful·ly
guile·ful·ness
guile·less
guilt·i·ly
guilt·i·ness
guilt·less·ly
guilt·less·ness
guilty
guise
gull·ibil·i·ty
gull·ible
gull·ibly
gun·man
gunned
gun·ning
gun·pow·der
gun·run·ner
gun·run·ning
gun·shot
gut·ter
gy·ne·co·log·i·cal
gy·ne·col·o·gist
gy·ne·col·o·gy
gy·rate
gy·rat·ed
gy·ra·tion
gy·ra·tion·al

ha·be·as cor·pus
ha·ben·dum et
  te·nen·dum
ha·be·re fa·ci·as
  pos·ses·si·o·nem
ha·be·re fa·ci·as
  sei·si·nam
hab·it·able·ness
hab·it·ably
hab·it·ancy
hab·it·ant
hab·i·ta·tion
ha·bit·u·al
ha·bit·u·al·ly
ha·bit·u·al·ness
ha·bit·u·ate
ha·bit·u·a·tion
half—breed
hal·lu·ci·nate
hal·lu·ci·na·tion·al
hal·lu·ci·na·tive
hal·lu·ci·na·to·ry
hal·lu·ci·no·gen·ic
ham·per
ham·pered
hand·bill
hand·cuff
hand·cuffed
hand·i·cap
hand·i·capped

hand·i·cap·ping
han·dle
han·dled
han·dler
han·dling
hand·writ·ing
hand·writ·ten
ha·rangue
ha·rangued
ha·rangu·ing
ha·rass
ha·rassed
ha·rass·ing
ha·rass·ment
har·bor
har·bored
hard·ship
harm·ful
harm·ful·ly
harm·ful·ness
harm·less
har·mo·ni·ous·ly
har·mo·ni·ous·ness
har·mo·nize
har·mo·ny
hash·ish
hatch·way
ha·tred
hawk·er
haz·ard·ous·ly
haz·ard·ous·ness
head·quar·ters
hear·ing
hear·say
heart·bro·ken
hect·are

hedge
hedged
hedg·er
heed
heed·ed
heed·less·ly
heed·less·ness
hei·nous
hei·nous·ly
hei·nous·ness
heir mas.
heir·ess fem.
heir·loom
heir·ship
he·ma·tol·o·gist
he·ma·to·ma
hemi·ple·gia
hemi·ple·gic
he·mo·glo·bin
hem·or·rhage
hem·or·rhaged
hem·or·rhag·ic
hem·or·rhag·ing
hence·forth
hence·for·ward
hench·man
hep·a·ti·tis
here·af·ter
here·by
he·red·i·ta·ble
her·e·dit·a·ments
he·red·i·tary
he·red·i·ty
here·in
here·in·above
here·in·af·ter

here·in·be·fore
here·of
he·res or
   hae·res
her·e·sy
her·e·tic
he·ret·i·cal·ly
here·to
here·to·fore
here·un·der
here·un·to
here·up·on
here·with
her·i·ta·bil·i·ty
her·i·ta·ble
her·i·tage
her·i·tance
her·i·tor
her·nia
her·ni·or·rha·phy
he·ro·ic
he·ro·ical·ly
her·o·in (drug)
her·o·ine (female)
her·o·ism
hes·i·tant
hes·i·tate
hes·i·tat·ed
hes·i·tat·ing
hes·i·ta·tion
het·er·o·ge·neous
hi·a·tus
hi·er·arch
hi·er·ar·chic
hi·er·ar·chi·cal
hi·er·ar·chy

high·way·man
hi·jack or
   high—jack
hi·jacked or
   high—jacked
hi·jack·er or
   high—jack·er
hi·jack·ing or
   high—jack·ing
hin·der
hin·dered
hin·drance
hit—and—run adj.
hith·er·to
hoax
hoc tit·u·lo
hoist·ed
hoist·er
hold·er
ho·lo·caust
ho·lo·graph
ho·lo·graph·ic
home·stead·er
ho·mi·ci·dal
ho·mi·ci·dal·ly
ho·mi·cide
ho·mol·o·gate
ho·mol·o·ga·tion
hon·or·able
hon·o·rar·ia pl.
hon·o·rar·i·um sing.
hon·or·ary
hon·ored
hon·or·er
hood·lum
hood·wink

horn·book
hor·ror
hos·pi·ta·ble
hos·pi·ta·bly
hos·pi·tal
hos·pi·tal·i·ty
hos·pi·tal·iza·tion
hos·pi·tal·ize
hos·pi·tal·ized
hos·tage
hos·tile
hos·til·i·ty
hotch·pot
ho·tel·keep·er
house·break·er
house·hold·er
house·keep·er
huck·ster
hu·man·i·tar·i·an
hu·mer·us (bone)
hu·mor·ous (witty)
hun·dred·weight
hur·ri·cane
hus·band
hy·brid
hy·brid·ism
hy·giene
hy·gien·ic
hy·gien·i·cal·ly
hy·gien·ist
hy·per·ac·tive
hy·per·ten·sion
hy·per·tro·phy
hyp·not·ic
hyp·not·i·cal·ly
hyp·no·tism

hyp·no·tist
hyp·no·tize
hyp·no·tized
hy·po·chon·dria
hy·po·chon·dri·ac
hy·po·chon·dri·a-
  cal·ly
hy·po·der·mic
hy·po·ten·sion
hy·poth·e·cate
hy·poth·e·ca·tion
hy·poth·e·ca·tor
hy·poth·e·ses pl.
hy·poth·e·sis sing.
hy·po·thet·ic
hy·po·thet·i·cal·ly
hys·ter·ec·to·my
hys·te·ria
hys·ter·i·cal·ly
hys·ter·ics

I

ibid. (abbreviation of
  ibidem)
id. (abbreviation of
  idem)
idem so·nans
iden·ti·cal·ly
iden·ti·fi·able

iden·ti·fi·ably
iden·ti·fi·ca·tion
iden·ti·fied
iden·ti·fy·ing
iden·ti·ty
id·io·path·ic
id·i·ot·ic
id·i·ot·i·cal·ly
i.e. (abbreviation of *id
  est*)
ig·nite
ig·nit·ed
ig·ni·tion
ig·no·min·i·ous·ly
ig·no·min·i·ous-
  ness
ig·no·mi·ny
ig·no·rance
ig·no·rant
ig·no·ran·tia
  le·gis
  nem·i·nem
  ex·cus·at
ig·no·rant·ly
il·i·ac
il·i·um
il·le·gal
il·le·gal·i·ty
il·le·gal·ly
il·leg·i·bil·i·ty
il·leg·i·ble
  (undecipherable; cf.
  eligible)
il·leg·i·bly
il·le·git·i·ma·cy
il·le·git·i·mate

il·le·git·i·mate·ly
il·lic·it (unlawful;
   cf. *elicit*)
il·lic·it·ly
il·lit·er·a·cy
il·lit·er·ate·ly
il·lit·er·ate·ness
ill·ness
il·log·i·cal
ill—us·age
il·lu·sion (deception;
   cf. *allusion, elusion*)
il·lu·sion·al
il·lu·sion·ary
il·lu·sive
il·lu·sive·ly
il·lu·sive·ness
il·lu·so·ry
imag·i·nary
imag·i·na·tion
imag·i·na·tive
imag·ine
imag·ined
imag·in·ing
im·be·cile
im·be·cil·i·ty
im·bro·glio
im·i·tate
im·i·tat·ed
im·i·ta·tion
im·i·ta·tive
im·ma·te·ri·al
im·ma·te·ri·al·ly
im·ma·te·ri·al·ness
im·ma·ture
im·ma·tur·i·ty

im·me·di·a·cy
im·me·di·ate·ly
im·me·mo·ri·al
im·mi·grant (one en-
   tering; cf. *emigrant*)
im·mi·grate (enter;
   cf. *emigrate*)
im·mi·grat·ed
im·mi·gra·tion
im·mi·nence
   (immediacy; cf.
   eminence)
im·mi·nent
   (impending; cf.
   eminent)
im·mi·nent·ly
im·mo·bi·li·za·tion
im·mo·bi·lize
im·mo·bi·liz·ed
im·mod·er·a·cy
im·mod·er·ate·ly
im·mod·er·ate·ness
im·mod·er·a·tion
im·mod·est·ly
im·mod·es·ty
im·mor·al
im·mor·al·ist
im·mo·ral·i·ty
im·mor·al·ly
im·mov·abil·i·ty
im·mov·able
im·mov·able·ness
im·mov·ably
im·mune
im·mu·ni·ty
im·pact

im·pair
im·paired
im·pair·er
im·pair·ment
im·pan·el
im·pan·eled
im·pan·el·ing
im·parl
im·par·lance
im·par·tial
im·par·tial·i·ty
im·par·tial·ly
im·peach·able
im·peached
im·peach·ment
im·pe·cu·ni·os·i·ty
im·pe·cu·nious
im·pe·cu·nious·ly
im·pe·cu·nious·ness
im·pede
im·ped·ed
im·ped·i·ment
im·ped·i·men·ta
im·ped·i·men·tal
im·ped·i·men·ta·ry
im·pend·ing
im·pen·i·tence
im·per·a·tive
im·per·a·tive·ly
im·per·a·tive·ness
im·per·fect
im·per·fec·tion
im·per·fect·ly
im·per·son·al·ly
im·per·son·ate
im·per·son·at·ed

im·per·son·at·ing
im·per·son·ation
im·per·son·ator
im·per·ti·nence
im·per·ti·nent·ly
im·pet·u·os·i·ty
im·pet·u·ous
im·pe·tus
im·pla·ca·ble
im·plau·si·bil·i·ty
im·plau·si·ble
im·plead
im·plead·able
im·plead·er
im·ple·ment
im·ple·men·tal
im·ple·men·ta·tion
im·ple·ment·ed
im·pli·cate
im·pli·cat·ed
im·pli·ca·tion
im·pli·ca·tive
im·pli·ca·tive·ly
im·plic·it
im·plic·it·ly
im·plied
im·ply·ing
im·plore
im·plored
im·port
im·port·able
im·por·tance
im·por·tant
im·por·tant·ly
im·por·ta·tion
im·port·ed

im·port·er
im·por·tu·nate
im·por·tu·nate·ly
im·por·tune
im·por·tu·ni·ty
im·pose
im·posed
im·pos·er
im·pos·ing·ly
im·po·si·tion
im·pos·si·bil·i·ty
im·pos·si·ble
im·pos·si·bly
im·post
im·pos·tor   *or*
   im·pos·ter
im·pos·ture
im·po·tence
im·po·ten·cy
im·po·tent
im·po·ten·tia
   ex·cus·at
   le·gem
im·pound·ed
im·pound·ment
im·pov·er·ish
im·pov·er·ished
im·prac·ti·ca·bil·i·ty
im·prac·ti·ca·ble
im·prac·ti·cal
im·prac·ti·cal·i·ty
im·prac·ti·cal·ness
im·pre·cise
im·pre·ci·sion
im·pre·scrip·ti·bil-
   i·ty

im·pre·scrip·ti·ble
im·pre·scrip·ti·bly
im·press
im·pressed
im·pres·sion
im·press·ment
im·pri·ma·tur
im·pris·on
im·pris·oned
im·pris·on·ment
im·prob·a·bil·i·ty
im·prob·a·ble
im·prob·a·ble·ness
im·prob·a·bly
im·pro·bi·ty
im·prop·er·ly
im·pro·pri·ety
im·prove·ment
im·prov·i·dence
im·prov·i·dent·ly
im·pru·dence
im·pru·dent·ly
im·pugn
im·pugned
im·pugn·ing
im·pulse
im·pul·sive·ly
im·pul·sive·ness
im·pu·ni·ty
im·put·able
im·put·ably
im·pu·ta·tive
im·pu·ta·tive·ly
im·pu·ta·tion
im·pute
in·ac·ces·si·bil·i·ty

in·ac·ces·si·ble
in·ac·ces·si·bly
in·ac·cu·ra·cy
in·ac·cu·rate·ly
in·ac·tive
in ac·tu
in·ad·e·qua·cy
in·ad·e·quate·ly
in·ad·e·quate·ness
in·ad·mis·si·bil·i·ty
in·ad·mis·si·ble
in·ad·mis·si·bly
in·ad·ver·tence
in·ad·ver·ten·cy
in·ad·ver·tent·ly
in·ad·vis·abil·i·ty
in·ad·vis·able
in·alien·abil·i·ty
in·alien·able
in·alien·ably
in·ap·pli·ca·ble
in·ap·pli·ca·bly
in·as·much as
in·au·gu·rate
in·au·gu·rat·ed
in·au·gu·ra·tion
in ban·co
in·cal·cu·la·ble
in cam·era
in·ca·pa·bil·i·ty
in·ca·pa·ble
in·ca·pac·i·tate
in·ca·pac·i·tat·ed
in·ca·pac·i·ta·tion
in·ca·pac·i·ty
in·car·cer·ate

in·car·cer·at·ed
in·car·cer·a·tion
in·cen·di·a·rism
in·cen·di·ary
in·cep·tion
in·cep·tive·ly
in·cest
in·ces·tu·ous
in·ces·tu·ous·ly
in·ces·tu·ous·ness
in·cho·ate
in·cho·ate·ly
in·cho·ate·ness
in·cho·ative·ly
in·ci·dence
in·ci·dent
in·ci·den·tal
in·ci·den·tal·ly
in·cip·i·ent
in·cite
in·cit·ed
in·cite·ment
in·cit·er
in·cli·na·tion
in·cline
in·clined
in·clude
in·clud·ed
in·clu·sion
in·clu·sive·ly
in·clu·sive·ness
in·cog·ni·to
in·co·her·ence
in·co·her·ent·ly
in com·men·dam
in·com·mu·ni·ca·do

in·com·mut·able
in·com·pat·i·bil·i·ty
im·com·pat·i·ble
in·com·pat·i·bly
in·com·pe·tence
in·com·pe·ten·cy
in·com·pe·tent·ly
in·com·pre·hen·si-
   ble
in·con·ceiv·able
in·con·ceiv·ably
in·con·clu·sive
in·con·clu·sive·ly
in·con·clu·sive·ness
in·con·for·mi·ty
in·con·gru·ous
in·con·se·quen·tial
in·con·sis·ten·cy
in·con·sis·tent·ly
in·con·test·abil·i·ty
in·con·test·able
in·con·test·ably
in·con·ti·nence
in·con·ti·nent
in·con·tro·vert·ible
in·con·tro·vert·ibly
in·con·ve·nience
in·con·ve·nient
in·cor·po·rate
in·cor·po·rat·ed
in·cor·po·ra·tion
in·cor·po·ra·tive
in·cor·po·ra·tor
in·cor·po·re·al
in·cor·po·re·al·ly
in·cor·ri·gi·bil·i·ty

in·cor·ri·gi·ble
in·cor·ri·gi·ble·ness
in·cor·ri·gi·bly
in·cor·rupt·ibil·i·ty
in·cor·rupt·ible
in·cor·rup·tion
in·creas·able
in·crease
in·creas·ing·ly
in·cred·i·ble
in·cred·i·bly
in·cre·du·li·ty
in·cred·u·lous·ly
in·cre·ment
in·cre·men·tal
in·crim·i·nate
in·crim·i·nat·ed
in·crim·i·nat·ing
in·crim·i·na·tion
in·crim·i·na·to·ry
in·cul·pa·ble
in·cul·pate
in·cul·pa·tion
in·cul·pa·to·ry
in·cum·ben·cy
in·cum·bent
in·cur
in·cur·abil·i·ty
in·cur·able
in·cur·able·ness
in·cur·ably
in cu·ria
in·curred
in·cur·ring
in cus·to·dia
  le·gis

in·de·bi·ta·tus
  as·sump·sit
in·debt·ed
in·debt·ed·ness
in·de·cen·cy
in·de·cent·ly
in·de·cent·ness
in·de·co·rum
in·de·fea·si·bil·i·ty
in·de·fea·si·ble
in·de·fea·si·bly
in·de·fen·si·ble
in·def·i·nite
in·def·i·nite·ly
in·def·i·nite·ness
in·dem·ni·fi·ca·tion
in·dem·ni·fied
in·dem·ni·fi·er
in·dem·ni·fy
in·dem·ni·fy·ing
in·dem·ni·tee
in·dem·ni·ties
in·dem·ni·tor
in·dem·ni·ty
in·den·ture
in·den·tured
in·de·pen·dence
in·de·pen·dent·ly
in·de·ter·min·able-
  ness
in·de·ter·min·ably
in·de·ter·mi·nate
in·de·ter·mi·na·tion
in·de·ter·min·ism
in·dex·es   *or*
  in·di·ces

in·di·cate
in·di·cat·ed
in·di·ca·tion
in·dic·a·tive
in·dic·a·tive·ly
in·di·cia
in·dict
in·dict·able
in·dict·ed
in·dict·ee
in·dict·er   *or*
  in·dict·or
in·dict·ing
in·dict·ment
in·dif·fer·ence
in·dif·fer·ent·ly
in·di·gence
in·di·gent
in·dig·nant·ly
in·dig·na·tion
in·dig·ni·ty
in·di·rect
in·di·rec·tion
in·di·rect·ly
in·di·rect·ness
in·dis·creet
in·dis·creet·ly
in·dis·creet·ness
in·dis·cre·tion
in·dis·crim·i·nate·ly
in·dis·pens·abil·i·ty
in·dis·pens·able
in·dis·pens·ably
in·dis·posed
in·dis·po·si·tion
in·dis·pu·ta·ble

in·dis·pu·ta·ble-
 ness
in·dis·pu·ta·bly
in·dis·tan·ter
in·dis·tin·guish·able
in·di·vid·u·al
in·di·vid·u·al·ism
in·di·vid·u·al·is·tic
in·di·vid·u·al·ly
in·di·vis·i·bil·i·ty
in·di·vis·i·ble
in·di·vis·i·ble·ness
in·di·vis·i·bly
in·di·vi·sion
in·dorse
in·du·bi·ta·bil·i·ty
in·du·bi·ta·ble
in·du·bi·ta·bly
in·duce
in·duced
in·duce·ment
in·duc·er
in·duc·ible
in·duc·ing
in·duct·ed
in·duct·ee
in·duc·tion
in·duc·tive·ly
in·dulge
in·dulged
in·dul·gence
in·dul·gent·ly
in·dulg·ing
in·du·rate
in·du·ra·tion
in·dus·tri·al

in·dus·tri·al·ist
in·dus·tri·al·iza·tion
in·dus·tri·al·ly
in·dus·try
ine·bri·ant
ine·bri·ate
ine·bri·at·ed
ine·bri·a·tion
in·ebri·ety
in·ef·fi·cien·cy
in·ef·fi·cient·ly
in·el·i·gi·bil·i·ty
in·el·i·gi·ble
in·equal·i·ty
in·eq·ui·ta·ble
in·eq·ui·ta·bly
in·eq·ui·ty (injustice;
 cf. *iniquity*)
in·es·cap·able
in·es·cap·ably
in es·se
in·ev·i·ta·bil·i·ty
in·ev·i·ta·ble
in·ev·i·ta·bly
in·ex·cus·able
in·ex·o·ra·bil·i·ty
in·ex·o·ra·ble
in·ex·pe·di·ent
in·ex·pe·ri·ence
in·ex·pli·ca·ble
in·ex·pli·ca·bly
in ex·ten·so
in ex·tre·mis
in fa·cie cu·ri·ae
in fac·to
in·fal·li·bil·i·ty

in·fal·li·ble
in·fal·li·bly
in·fa·mous
in·fa·mous·ly
in·fa·my
in·fan·cy
in·fant
in·fan·ti·cide
in·fan·tile
in·fan·til·ism
in·farct
in·fat·u·at·ed
in·fat·u·a·tion
in·fect·ed
in·fec·tion
in·fec·tious
in·feoff·ment
in·fer
in·fer·ence
in·fer·en·tial
in·fer·en·tial·ly
in·fe·ri·or
in·fe·ri·or·i·ty
in·fe·ri·or·ly
in·ferred
in·fer·ring
in·fi·del
in·fi·del·i·ties
in·fi·del·i·ty
in·firm
in·fir·mi·ty
in fla·gran·te
 de·lic·to
in·flam·ma·tion
in·flam·ma·to·ry
in·fla·tion·ary

60

in·fla·tion·ism
in·fla·tion·ist
in·flex·i·ble
in·flict·ed
in·flic·tion
in·flic·tive
in·flic·tor
in·flu·ence
in·flu·en·tial
in·for·mal
in·for·mal·i·ty
in·for·mal·ly
in·for·mant
in for·ma
   pau·pe·ris
in·for·ma·tion·al
in·for·ma·tive
in·for·ma·to·ry
in·formed
in·form·er
in·fra
in·frac·tion
in frau·dem
   le·gis
in·fringe
in·fringed
in·fringe·ment
in·fring·er
in fu·tu·ro
in·ge·nious
in·ge·nu·ity
in·gen·u·ous·ly
in·grat·i·tude
in·gress
in·gres·sion
in·gui·nal

in·hab·it·able
in·hab·i·tant
in·hab·it·ed
in hac par·te
in haec ver·ba
in·here
in·her·ence
in·her·en·cy
in·her·ent·ly
in·her·it
in·her·it·able
in·her·i·tance
in·her·it·ed
in·her·i·tor mas.
in·her·i·tress fem.
in·her·i·trix fem.
in·hib·it·ed
in·hi·bi·tion
in·hib·i·tive
in·hib·i·tor or
   in·hib·i·ter
in·hib·i·to·ry
in hoc
in·hu·man
in·hu·mane
in·hu·mane·ly
in·hu·man·ly
in in·vi·tum
in·iq·ui·tous
in·iq·ui·ty (sin; cf.
   inequity)
ini·tial
ini·tialed or
   ini·tialled
ini·tial·ly
ini·tiate n., adj.

ini·ti·ate v.
ini·ti·at·ed
ini·ti·a·tion
ini·tia·tive
in in·i·tio
in ju·di·cio
in·ju·di·cious
in·junc·tion
in·junc·tive
in ju·re
in·jure
in·jured
in·jur·er
in·ju·ria abs·que
   dam·no
in·ju·ries
in·ju·ri·ous
in·ju·ri·ous·ly
in·ju·ry
in·jus·tice
in lieu
in limine
in li·tem
in lo·co
   pa·ren·tis
in·mate
in me·di·as res
in·nate
in·no·cence
in·no·cent
in·no·cent·ly
in·nom·i·nate
in·no·va·tion
in·nu·en·do sing.
in·nu·en·dos or
   in·nu·en·does pl.

61

in·nu·mer·a·ble
in·op·por·tune
in·or·di·nate·ly
in pais
in pa·ri cau·sa
in pa·ri de·lic·to
in pa·ri
 ma·te·ria
in pa·ri pas·su
in pec·to·re
in pen·den·te
in per·pe·tu·um
in per·so·nam
in prae·sen·ti
in pri·mis
in prin·ci·pio
in pro·pria
 per·so·na
in prox·i·mo
 gra·du
in·quest
in·quire
in·quired
in·qui·ry
in·qui·si·tion
in·quis·i·tive·ness
in·quis·i·tor
in re
in rem
in re·rum
 na·tu·ra
in·sane·ly
in·sane·ness
in·san·i·ty
in·scribe
in·scribed

in·scrib·er
in·scrip·tion
in·se·cure·ly
in·se·cure·ness
in·se·cu·ri·ty
in·sen·si·bil·i·ty
in·sen·si·ble
in·sep·a·ra·ble
in·sid·i·ous
in·sig·nia
in·sig·nif·i·cance
in·sig·nif·i·cant·ly
in·sin·cere
in·sin·cer·i·ty
in·sin·u·ate
in·sin·u·at·ed
in·sin·u·a·tion
in·sin·u·a·tive
in·sist·ed
in·sis·tence
in si·tu
in·so·far as
in·so·lence
in·so·lent·ly
in·solv·able
in·sol·ven·cy
in·sol·vent
in spe·cie
in·spect
in·spec·ta·tor
in·spect·ed
in·spec·tion
in·spec·tor
in·sta·bil·i·ty
in·stall or
 in·stal

in·stal·la·tion
in·stalled
in·stall·ing
in·stall·ment or
 in·stal·ment
in·stance
in·stant
in·stan·ta·neous·ly
in·stan·ter
in·stant·ly
in sta·tu quo
in·sti·gate
in·sti·gat·ed
in·sti·ga·tion
in·sti·ga·tive
in·sti·ga·tor
in stir·pes
in·sti·tute
in·sti·tut·ed
in·sti·tut·er or
 in·sti·tut·or
in·sti·tu·tion·al·ly
in stric·to ju·re
in·struct·ed
in·struc·tion·al
in·struc·tive
in·struc·tor
in·stru·ment
in·stru·men·tal
in·stru·men·tal·i·ty
in·stru·men·tal·ly
in·stru·men·ta·tion
in·sub·or·di·nate
in·sub·or·di·na·tion
in·suf·fer·able
in·suf·fi·cien·cy

in·suf·fi·cient·ly
in·su·late
in·su·lat·ed
in·su·la·tion
in·su·la·tor
in·su·per·a·ble
in·sup·port·able
in·sur·abil·i·ty
in·sur·able
in·sur·ance
in·sure
in·sured
in·sur·er
in·sur·gence
in·sur·gen·cy
in·sur·gent
in·sur·mount·able
in·sur·rec·tion
in sus·pen·so
in·tan·gi·bil·i·ty
in·tan·gi·ble
in·tan·gi·bly
in tan·tum
in·te·gral
in·te·gral·ly
in·te·grate
in·te·grat·ed
in·te·gra·tion
in·te·gra·tor
in·teg·ri·ty
in·tel·lect
in·tel·lec·tu·al
in·tel·li·gence
in·tel·li·gent·ly
in·tel·li·gi·bil·i·ty
in·tel·li·gi·ble

in·tel·li·gi·bly
in·tem·per·ance
in·tem·per·ate
in·tend·ed
in·tend·ment
in·ten·si·fi·ca·tion
in·ten·si·fied
in·ten·si·fy
in·ten·si·fy·ing
in·tent
in·ten·tion
in·ten·tion·al
in·ten·tion·al·ly
in·ter
in·ter·ac·tion
in·ter alia
in·ter ali·os
    ac·ta
in·ter·cede
in·ter·ced·ed
in·ter·ced·er
in·ter·cept·ed
in·ter·cep·tion
in·ter·cep·tive
in·ter·cep·tor
in·ter·ces·sion
in·ter·change
in·ter·change·able
in·ter·change·ably
in·ter·cos·tal
in·ter·course
in·ter·dict
in·ter·dict·ed
in·ter·dic·tion
in·ter·dic·tive
in·ter·dic·tor

in·ter·dic·to·ry
in·ter·est
in·ter·est·ed
in·ter·fere
in·ter·fered
in·ter·fer·ence
in·ter·fer·en·tial
in·ter·fer·er
in·ter·fer·ing
in·ter·im
in·te·ri·or
in·ter·jec·tion
in·ter·line
in·ter·lin·ear
in·ter·lin·e·ate
in·ter·lin·ea·tion
in·ter·loc·u·tor
in·ter·loc·u·to·ry
in·ter·lope
in·ter·lop·er
in·ter·mar·riage
in·ter·mar·ry
in·ter·me·di·ary
in·ter·me·di·ate
in·ter·me·di·a·tion
in·ter·ment
in·ter·mit·tent·ly
in·tern
in·ter·nal·ly
in·ter·na·tion·al·ly
in·ter·ne·cine
in·tern·ee
in·ter·nist
in·ter nos
in·ter·pel·late
in·ter·pel·la·tion

in·ter·pel·la·tor
in·ter·plea
in·ter·plead
in·ter·plead·ed
in·ter·plead·er
in·ter·po·late
in·ter·po·lat·ed
in·ter·po·la·tion
in·ter·po·la·tive
in·ter·po·la·tor
in·ter·pose
in·ter·pos·er
in·ter·po·si·tion
in·ter·pret
in·ter·pre·ta·tion
in·ter·pre·ta·tion·al
in·ter·pre·ta·tive·ly
in·ter·pret·ed
in·ter·pret·er
in·ter·ra·cial
in·terred
in·ter·re·late
in·ter·re·lat·ed
in·ter·re·la·tion·ship
in·ter·ring
in·ter·ro·gate
in·ter·ro·gat·ed
in·ter·ro·ga·tion
in·ter·rog·a·tive·ly
in·ter·rog·a·tor
in·ter·rog·a·to·ries
in·ter·rog·a·to·ry
in   ter·ro·rem
in·ter·rupt·ed
in·ter·rupt·er
in·ter·rup·tion

in·ter·rup·tive
in·ter   se
in·ter·sect·ed
in·ter·sec·tion·al
in·ter·state (between
    states; cf. *intrastate*)
in·ter·sti·tial
in·ter·twined
in·ter·vene
in·ter·vened
in·ter·ve·nor
in·ter·ven·tion
in·ter·ver·te·bral
in·ter   vi·rum
    et   ux·orem
in·ter   vi·vos
in·tes·ta·ble
in·tes·ta·cy
in·tes·tate
in·ti·ma·cy
in·ti·mate
in·ti·mat·ed
in·ti·mate·ly
in·ti·mate·ness
in·ti·ma·tion
in·tim·i·date
in·tim·i·dat·ed
in·tim·i·da·tion
in·tim·i·da·tor
in·tol·er·a·bil·i·ty
in·tol·er·a·ble
in·tol·er·a·bly
in·tol·er·ance
in·tol·er·ant·ly
in   to·to
in·tox·i·cant

in·tox·i·cate
in·tox·i·cat·ed
in·tox·i·ca·tion
in·trac·ta·ble
in·tra·li·min·al
in·tra·mus·cu·lar·ly
in·tran·si·gent
in   tran·si·tu
in·tra·state (within a
    state; cf. *interstate*)
in·tra·ve·nous·ly
in·tra   vi·res
in·tri·ca·cy
in·tri·cate
in·trigue
in·trigued
in·trin·sic
in·trin·si·cal·ly
in·tro·duce
in·tro·duced
in·tro·duc·tion
in·tro·duc·to·ri·ly
in·tro·duc·to·ry
in·trude
in·trud·ed
in·trud·er
in·tru·sion
in·tru·sive·ly
in·tru·sive·ness
in·tu·i·tu
    ma·tri·mo·nii
in·tu·i·tu   mor·tis
in   vin·cu·lis
in   vi·ta
ip·se   dix·it
ip·so   fac·to

ip·so ju·re
ir·re·claim·able
ir·rec·on·cil·abil·i·ty
ir·rec·on·cil·able
ir·re·cov·er·able
ir·re·cu·sa·ble
ir·re·deem·able
ir·ref·ra·ga·ble

J

jac·ti·ta·tion
jac·tus
jailed
jail·er or
   jail·or
jeal·ous·ly
jeal·ous·ness
jeal·ou·sy
jeop·ar·dize
jeop·ar·dized
jeop·ar·dy
jet·sam
jet·ti·son
jew·el·er or
   jew·el·ler
jew·el·ry
job·ber

join·der
joint·ed
joint·ly
join·tress
join·ture
jos·tle
jos·tled
jos·tling
jour·nal
jour·ney
jour·neyed
jour·ney·man
judge
judged
judg·ing
judg·ment or
   judge·ment
ju·di·ca·tio
ju·di·ca·ture
ju·di·cial
ju·di·cial·ly
ju·di·cia·ry
ju·di·cious
ju·di·cious·ly
ju·di·cious·ness
ju·nior
jur·al
jur·al·ly
ju·ra
   per·so·na·rum
ju·ra re·rum
ju·rat
ju·ra·tion
ju·re ci·vi·li
ju·re ux·o·ris
ju·rid·i·cal

ju·ris
ju·ris·dic·tion
ju·ris·dic·tion·al
ju·ris·pru·dence
ju·ris·pru·dent
ju·rist
ju·ror
ju·ry
ju·ry·man
jus ab·u·ten·di
jus ac·cre·scen·di
jus ad rem
jus ci·vi·le
jus com·mer·cii
jus com·mu·ne
jus dis·po·nen·di
jus fru·en·di
jus gen·ti·um
jus ha·ben·di
jus in
   per·so·nam
jus in re
jus pro·pri·e·ta·tis
jus·tice
jus·tic·es
jus·tice·ship
jus·ti·fi·able
jus·ti·fi·ably
jus·ti·fi·ca·tion
jus·ti·fied
jus·ti·fy·ing
just·ly
just·ness
ju·ve·nile
ju·ve·nil·i·ty
jux·ta·po·si·tion

K

L

kan·ga·roo
ker·o·sine *or*
  ker·o·sene
key·note
kick·back n.
kid·nap
kid·napped *or*
  kid·naped
kid·nap·per *or*
  kid·nap·er
kid·nap·ping *or*
  kid·nap·ing
kin
kin·der·gart·ner
kin·dred
ki·net·ic
kin·folk *or*
  kins·folk
kin·ship
kins·man
kins·wo·man
klep·to·ma·nia
klep·to·ma·ni·ac
knell
know—how
know·ing·ly
know—it—all
knowl·edge
knowl·edge·able
knowl·edge·ably

la·bel
la·bel·ed *or*
  la·belled
la·bel·ing *or*
  la·bel·ling
la·bor·er
la·ches
la·ity
land·lord
land·mark
lap·page
lapse
lapsed
laps·ing
lar·ce·nist
lar·ce·nous
lar·ce·ny
las·civ·i·ous
las·civ·i·ous·ly
la·ten·cy
la·tent·ly
law·ful
law·ful·ly
law·ful·ness
law·less·ly
law·less·ness
law·suit
law·yer
lay·man
lay·off n.

lay off v.
league
lease
leased
lease·hold
lease·hold·er
leas·es
led·ger
leg·a·cy
le·gal
le·gal·ism
le·gal·ist
le·gal·is·tic
le·gal·is·ti·cal·ly
le·gal·i·ty
le·gal·iza·tion
le·gal·ize
le·gal·ized
le·gal·ly
leg·ate n.
le·gate v.
leg·a·tee
le·ga·tion
leg·is·late
leg·is·lat·ed
leg·is·la·tion
leg·is·la·tive
leg·is·la·tor
leg·is·la·ture
le·git·i·ma·cy
le·git·i·mate·ly
le·git·i·ma·tion
le·git·i·mize
lend·er
le·sion
les·see

less·er adj.
les·sor n.
le·thal
let·ting
le·va·ri fa·ci·as
lev·i·able
lev·ied
lev·i·er
lev·ies
levy
lev·y·ing
lewd·ness
lex
  com·mis·so·ria
lex do·mi·ci·lii
lex fo·ri
lex lo·ci ac·tus
lex lo·ci
  con·trac·tus
lex lo·ci
  de·lic·ti
lex lo·ci
  rei si·tae
lex non
  scrip·ta
li·a·bil·i·ties
li·a·bil·i·ty
li·a·ble (likely)
li·ai·son
li·bel (defame)
li·bel·ant or
  li·bel·lant
li·beled or
  li·belled
li·bel·ee
  or li·bel·lee

li·bel·ing or
  li·bel·ling
li·bel·ous or
  li·bel·lous
li·ber (pl.: libri)
lib·er·al
lib·er·al·i·ty
lib·er·al·iza·tion
lib·er·al·ize
lib·er·al·ized
lib·er·al·ly
lib·er·ate
lib·er·at·ed
lib·er·a·tion
lib·er·ty
li·bri (sing.: liber)
li·cense
li·censed
li·cens·ee
li·cens·er or
  li·cen·sor
li·cens·es
li·cens·ing
li·cen·tious·ly
li·cen·tious·ness
lic·it
lic·i·ta·tion
lic·it·ly
lien
lien·or
lieu
lieu·ten·an·cy
lieu·ten·ant
light·er n. (barge)
light·er n., adj.
ligh·ter·age

ligh·ter·man
light·house
like·li·hood
like·ly
like·wise
lim·it
lim·i·ta·tion
lim·it·ed
lim·it·ed·ly
lim·it·less
lin·eage
lin·eal
liq·uid
liq·ui·date
liq·ui·dat·ed
liq·ui·da·tion
liq·ui·da·tor
li·quor
lis pen·dens
lit·er·al (verbatim; cf. littoral)
lit·er·al·ly
lit·er·al·ness
lit·er·ate·ly
lit·i·gant
lit·i·gate
lit·i·gat·ed
lit·i·ga·tion
li·ti·gious
li·ti·gious·ly
lit·to·ral (seaside; cf. literal)
lob·bied
lob·by
lob·by·er
lob·by·ing

lob·by·ist
lo·cal adj., n.
lo·cale n. (place)
lo·cal·ly
lo·cate
lo·cat·ed
lo·ca·tion
lo·ca·tion·al
loc·a·tive
lo·ci (sing.: *locus*)
lock·out n.
lock out v.
lo·co·mo·tive
lo·cum te·nens
  sing.
lo·cum
  te·nen·tes pl.
lo·cus (pl.: *loci*)
lo·cus
  con·trac·tus
lo·cus de·lic·ti
lo·cus in quo
lo·cus si·gil·li
  (abbrev.: L.S.)
lo·cus stan·di
lode
lodge
lodged
lodg·er
lodg·ing
logged
log·ging
log·ic
log·i·cal
log·i·cal·ly
loi·ter

loi·tered
loi·ter·er
lon·gev·i·ty
long·shore·man
look·out n.
look out v.
lot·ter·ies
lot·tery
loy·al·ist
loy·al·ly
loy·al·ty
lu·cid
lu·cid·i·ty
lu·cid·ly
lu·cid·ness
lu·cra·tive·ly
lu·na·cy
lu·na·tic
lurch
lynch
lynched
lynch·er

mach·i·na·tion
mach·i·na·tor
ma·chine
ma·chine·ry
ma·chin·ist

mad·man
mad·ness
mad·wom·an
mag·is·te·ri·al
mag·is·te·ri·al·ly
mag·is·tra·cy
mag·is·trate
mag·is·trat·i·cal
mail·able
maimed
maim·er
main·our *or*
  man·ner
main·per·na·ble
main·per·nor
main·prise
main·pri·sor
main·tain·able
main·tained
main·tain·er
main·te·nance
ma·jor
ma·jor·i·ty
mal·ad·just·ed
ma·la fi·des
ma·la in se
ma·la prax·is
ma·la pro·hi·bi·ta
mal·con·duct
mal·con·tent
male·fac·tion
male·fac·tor
ma·lef·ic
ma·lef·i·cence
ma·lef·i·cent
ma·lev·o·lence

ma·lev·o·lent
mal·fea·sance
mal·ice
ma·li·cious·ly
ma·li·cious·ness
ma·lign
ma·lig·nant
ma·ligned
ma·lign·ing
ma·lin·ger
ma·lin·gered
ma·lin·ger·er
mal·lea·bil·i·ty
mal·lea·ble
ma·lo an·i·mo
mal·prac·tice
mal·prac·ti·tion·er
mal·treat·ment
ma·lum in se
ma·lum
   pro·hi·bi·tum
man·age·abil·i·ty
man·age·able
man·age·able·ness
man·age·ably
man·age·ment
man·ag·er
man·a·ge·ri·al
man·da·mus
man·date
man·da·tor
man·da·to·ry
man·di·ble
ma·neu·ver
ma·neu·vered
man·hood

man—hours
man·hunt
ma·nia
ma·ni·ac
ma·ni·a·cal·ly
man·ic
man·i·fest
man·i·fes·ta·tion
man·i·fes·ta·tive
man·i·fest·ed
man·i·fest·ly
man·i·fes·to sing.
man·i·fes·tos or
   man·i·fes·toes pl.
ma·nip·u·late
ma·nip·u·lat·ed
ma·nip·u·la·tion
ma·nip·u·la·tive
ma·nip·u·la·tor
man·nire
man·slaugh·ter
man·slay·er
man·u·al·ly
man·u·fac·to·ry
man·u·fac·ture
man·u·fac·tured
man·u·fac·tur·er
ma·nu for·ti
ma·raud·er
mar·i·jua·na or
   mar·i·hua·na
ma·rine
mar·i·ner
mar·i·tal (of marriage;
   cf. *marshal, martial*)
mar·i·tal·ly

mar·i·time
mar·ket·abil·i·ty
mar·ket·able
mar·ket·ed
mar·ke·teer
marks·man·ship
mar·riage
mar·riage·able
mar·ried
mar·ry·ing
mar·shal (usher; cf.
   marital, martial)
mar·shaled or
   mar·shalled
mar·shal·ing or
   mar·shal·ling
mar·tial (warlike; cf.
   marital, marshal)
mar·tial·ly
mar·tyr
mar·tyr·dom
mar·tyred
mas·och·ism
mas·och·ist
mas·och·is·tic
mas·quer·ade
mas·quer·ad·ed
mas·sa·cre
mas·sa·cred
mas·sa·cring
mas·ter
mas·tered
mas·ter·ful·ly
mas·tery
ma·ter·fa·mil·i·as
ma·te·ri·al·ism

ma·te·ri·al·is·tic
ma·te·ri·al·is·ti·cal-
  ly
ma·te·ri·al·ize
ma·te·ri·al·ly
ma·te·ri·al·ness
ma·ter·nal
ma·ter·nal·ism
ma·ter·nal·ly
ma·ter·ni·ty
ma·tri·arch
ma·tri·ci·dal
ma·tri·cide
mat·ri·mo·nial
mat·ri·mo·nial·ly
mat·ri·mo·ny
ma·tron
ma·tron·ly
mat·ter
mat·u·ra·tion
ma·tured
ma·tu·ri·ty
max·il·la
max·im
max·i·mal
max·i·mal·ly
max·i·mum
may·hem
may·or·al
may·or·al·ty
may·or·ess fem.
me·an·der
me·an·dered
mea·sur·able
mea·sur·ably
mea·sure

mea·sured
mea·sure·ment
me·chan·ic
me·chan·i·cal·ly
mech·a·nism
me·di·ate
me·di·at·ed
me·di·ate·ly
me·di·a·tion
me·di·a·tor
me·di·a·tress fem.
med·i·cal
med·i·ca·tion
me·dic·i·nal
med·i·cine
me·di·o·cre
me·di·oc·ri·ty
me·di·um sing.
me·di·ums or
  me·dia pl.
meg·a·lo·ma·nia
mel·an·cho·lia
mel·an·chol·ic
mel·an·choly
mem·ber·ship
mem·o·ran·dum
  sing.
mem·o·ran·dums or
  mem·o·ran·da pl.
me·mo·ri·al
me·mo·ri·al·ize
mem·o·ri·za·tion
mem·o·rize
mem·o·rized
mem·o·ry
men·ace

men·aced
men·ac·ing·ly
men·da·cious
me·nial
me·nial·ly
men·sa et tho·ro
mens rea
men·tal
men·tal·i·ty
men·tal·ly
mer·can·tile
mer·can·til·ism
mer·can·til·is·tic
mer·ce·nary
mer·chan·dise
mer·chan·dis·er
mer·chant·abil·i·ty
mer·chant·able
mer·chant·man
mer·ci·less·ly
mer·cy
merge
merged
mer·gence
merg·er
mer·it
mer·it·ed
mer·i·to·ri·ous·ly
mesne
mes·sage
mes·sen·ger
mes·suage
me·tab·o·lism
meta·car·pal
meta·car·pus
meta·phys·i·cal

meta·phys·ics
meta·tar·sal
me·ter
meth·od
me·thod·i·cal·ly
met·ric
met·ri·cal·ly
me·trop·o·lis
met·ro·pol·i·tan
mi·cro·phone
mi·cro·scope
mi·cro·scop·ic
mid·dle·man
mid·wife
mi·grant
mile·age
mile·stone
mil·i·tan·cy
mil·i·tant
mil·i·tant·ly
mil·i·tant·ness
mil·i·ta·rism
mil·i·ta·rist
mil·i·ta·ris·tic
mil·i·ta·ri·za·tion
mil·i·ta·rize
mil·i·tary
mi·li·tia
mind·ful
mind·ful·ly
min·er (mine worker;
   cf. *minor*)
min·er·al
min·i·mal
min·i·mal·ly
min·i·mize

min·i·mum
min·is·ter
min·is·te·ri·al·ly
min·is·try
mi·nor (one under le-
   gal age; cf. *miner*)
mi·nor·i·ty
min·ute (time)
mi·nute (small)
mis·ad·ven·ture
mis·al·lege
mis·al·li·ance
mis·ap·pli·ca·tion
mis·ap·ply
mis·ap·pro·pri·ate
mis·ap·pro·pri·a-
   tion
mis·be·have
mis·be·haved
mis·be·hav·er
mis·be·hav·ior
mis·cal·cu·late
mis·cal·cu·la·tion
mis·car·riage
mis·car·ry
mis·ce·ge·na·tion
mis·cel·la·neous
mis·cel·la·ny
mis·charge
mis·chief
mis·con·duct
mis·cre·ant
mis·date
mis·de·liv·ery
mis·de·mean·ant
mis·de·mean·or

mis·di·rect
mis·di·rec·tion
mis·fea·sance
mis·fea·sor
mis·for·tune
mis·guid·ed
mis·han·dle
mis·in·for·ma·tion
mis·in·ter·pret
mis·in·ter·pre·ta-
   tion
mis·in·ter·pret·ed
mis·join·der
mis·lay
mis·man·age·ment
mis·no·mer
mis·pri·sion
mis·re·cit·al
mis·rep·re·sent
mis·rep·re·sen·ta-
   tion
mis·rep·re·sent·ed
mis·state
mis·stat·ed
mis·state·ment
mis·take
mis·tak·en
mis·took
mis·treat·ed
mis·treat·ment
mis·tri·al
mis·un·der·stand
mis·un·der·stood
mis·us·age
mis·use
mis·used

mis·us·er
mit·i·gate
mit·i·gat·ed
mit·i·gat·ing
mit·i·ga·tion
mit·i·ga·tive
mit·i·ga·tor
mit·i·ga·to·ry
mit·ti·mus
mobbed
mob·bing
mo·bile
mo·bi·li·za·tion
mo·bi·lize
mo·bi·lized
mo·bi·liz·ing
mod·el
mod·eled *or*
  mod·elled
mod·el·ing *or*
  mod·el·ling
mod·er·ate
mod·er·ate·ly
mod·er·ate·ness
mod·er·a·tion
mod·er·a·tor
mod·ern·iza·tion
mod·ern·iza·tion·al
mod·ern·ize
mod·ern·ized
mod·i·fi·able·ness
mod·i·fi·ca·tion
mod·i·fied
mod·i·fi·er
mod·i·fy
mo·do et for·ma

mo·dus ope·ran·di
mo·dus vi·ven·di
moi·ety
mold·er
mol·li·fied
mol·li·fy
mo·ment
mo·men·tar·i·ly
mo·men·tary
mon·e·tar·i·ly
mon·e·tary
mon·ey sing.
mon·eyed *or*
  mon·ied
mon·eys *or*
  mon·ies pl.
mo·ni·tion
mon·i·tor
mon·i·tored
mon·i·to·ry
mo·nog·a·mous
mo·nog·a·my
mo·nop·o·lies
mo·nop·o·list
mo·nop·o·lis·ti·cal-
  ly
mo·nop·o·li·za·tion
mo·nop·o·lize
mo·nop·o·lized
mo·nop·o·liz·er
mo·nop·o·ly
mon·strous
mon·u·ment
mon·u·men·tal
moot
mor·al (ethical)

mo·rale (attitude)
mor·al·ist
mor·al·is·tic
mo·ral·i·ty
mor·al·ly
mor·a·to·ri·um
mor·bid
more·over
morgue
mor·i·bund
mo·ron
mor·phine
mort
mor·tal
mor·tal·i·ty
mor·tal·ly
mort·gage
mort·gaged
mort·gag·ee
mort·gag·es
mort·ga·gor
mor·tis cau·sa
mor·tu·ary
moth·er·less
mo·tion
mo·tioned
mo·tion·less·ly
mo·tion·less·ness
mo·ti·vate
mo·ti·vat·ed
mo·ti·va·tion
mo·tive
mou·lage
moun·te·bank
mov·abil·i·ty *or*
  move·abil·i·ty

mov·able *or*
  move·able
mov·able·ness
mov·ably
mov·ant *or*
  mov·ent
move·ment
mu·cous adj.
mu·cus n.
mugged
mug·ger
mug·ging
mu·lat·to sing.
mu·lat·toes *or*
  mu·lat·tos pl.
mulct
mul·ti·far·i·ous·ly
mul·ti·far·i·ous·ness
mul·ti·lat·er·al
mul·ti·par·tite
mul·ti·ple
mul·ti·ply
mul·ti·tude
mul·ti·tu·di·nous·ly
mul·to for·ti·o·ri
mu·nic·i·pal
mu·nic·i·pal·i·ty
mu·nic·i·pal·ly
mu·ni·ments
mu·ni·tions
mur·der
mur·dered
mur·der·er mas.
mur·der·ess fem.
mur·der·ous·ly

mus·ter
mus·tered
mu·ti·late
mu·ti·lat·ed
mu·ti·la·tion
mu·ti·la·tor
mu·ti·neer
mu·ti·nous·ly
mu·ti·ny
mu·tua (sing.:
  mutuum)
mu·tu·al
mu·tu·al·i·ty
mu·tu·al·iza·tion
mu·tu·al·ly
mu·tu·um (pl.:
  mutua)
my·o·pia
my·o·pic
mys·te·ri·ous·ly
mys·te·ri·ous·ness
mys·tery

na·ked·ly
na·ked·ness
name·less·ly
name·ly

nar·co·sis
nar·cot·ic
na·scence
na·tion·al
na·tion·al·ist
na·tion·al·is·tic
na·tion·al·i·ty
na·tion·al·iza·tion
na·tion·al·ize
na·tive
na·tive·ly
nat·u·ral
nat·u·ral·iza·tion
nat·u·ral·ize
nat·u·ral·ized
nat·u·ral·ly
nat·u·ral·ness
na·val (shipping)
nav·i·ga·ble
nav·i·ga·bly
nav·i·gate
nav·i·gat·ed
nav·i·ga·tion·al
na·vy
nec·es·sar·i·ly
nec·es·sary
ne·ces·si·tate
ne·ces·si·tat·ed
ne·ces·si·ty
nec·rop·sy
née *or* nee
need·ful·ness
need·less
needy
ne·glect
ne·glect·ed

73

ne·glect·ful
ne·glect·ful·ly
ne·glect·ful·ness
neg·li·gence
neg·li·gi·bil·i·ty
neg·li·gi·ble
neg·li·gi·bly
ne·go·tia·ble
ne·go·ti·ate
ne·go·ti·at·ed
ne·go·ti·a·tion
ne·go·ti·a·tor
ne·mo
neo·plasm
neo·plas·tic
ner·vous·ly
ner·vous·ness
neu·ral
neur·as·the·nia
neu·ri·tis
neu·ro·log·i·cal
neu·rol·o·gist
neu·ro·ses pl.
neu·ro·sis sing.
neu·rot·ic
neu·tral
neu·tral·ism
neu·tral·is·tic
neu·tral·i·ty
neu·tral·iza·tion
neu·tral·ize
neu·tral·ized
neu·tral·iz·er
neu·tral·ly
ne va·ri·e·tur
ni·hil di·cit

ni·hil est
ni·hil ha·bet
ni·hil·ism
ni·hil·ist
ni·hil·is·tic
nil de·bet
ni·si pri·us
nol·le pro·se·qui
no·lo
   con·ten·de·re
no·men sing.
nom·i·na pl.
nom·i·nal
nom·i·nal·ly
nom·i·nate
nom·i·nat·ed
nom·i·na·tion
nom·i·na·tor
nom·i·nee
non·abil·i·ty
non·ac·cep·tance
non·ac·cess
non·ad·mis·sion
non·ap·pear·ance
non·as·sess·able
non as·sump·sit
non·can·cel·a·ble
non com·ba·tant
non com·pos
   men·tis
non con·stat
non·con·test·able
non·de·duct·ible
non·de·liv·ery
non·de·script
non·di·rec·tion

non·dis·clo·sure
non est fac·tum
non est
   in·ven·tus
non·fea·sance
non·for·feit·able
non·in·ter·ven·tion
non·join·der
non·ju·di·cial
non·lev·i·able
non·mail·able
non·mar·i·time
non·nav·i·ga·ble
non·ne·go·tia·ble
non ob·stan·te
   ve·re·dic·to
non·pay·ment
non·per·for·mance
non·prof·it
non
   pro·se·qui·tur
   (abbrev.: *non pros.*)
non·quo·ta
non·res·i·dent
non·sense
non se·qui·tur
non·suit
non·sup·port
non·us·er
non·waiv·er
nor·mal
nor·mal·i·ty
nor·mal·ly
nos·trum
no·ta be·ne
   (abbrev.: *N.B.*)

no·tar·i·al
no·ta·ries pub·lic
   or no·ta·ry
   pub·lics pl.
no·ta·ri·za·tion
no·ta·rize
no·ta·rized
no·ta·ry pub·lic
   sing.
no·ta·tion
no·tice
no·tic·es
no·ti·fi·ca·tion
no·ti·fied
no·ti·fy·ing
no·to·ri·ety
no·to·ri·ous
no·to·ri·ous·ly
no·to·ri·ous·ness
not·with·stand·ing
no·va·tion
nox·ious
nox·ious·ly
nu·da pac·ta pl.
nu·dum pac·tum
   sing.
nu·ga·tory
nui·sance
null
nul·la bo·na
nul·li·fi·ca·tion
nul·li·fied
nul·li·fy
nul·li·fy·ing
nul·li·ty
nul·li·us ju·ris

nul tort
nunc pro tunc
nun·cu·pate
nun·cu·pa·tive
nup·tial
nym·pho·ma·nia
nym·pho·ma·ni·ac
nys·tag·mus

oath
obe·di·ence
obe·di·ent
obe·di·en·tia
obei·sant
obey·ance (compli-
   ance; cf. *abeyance*)
obeyed
obey·ing
obi·ter dic·tum
ob·ject·ed
ob·jec·tion
ob·jec·tion·able
ob·jec·tive·ly
ob·jec·tive·ness
ob·jec·tiv·i·ty
ob·jec·tor
ob·li·gate
ob·li·gat·ed

ob·li·ga·tion
oblig·a·to·ry
ob·li·gee
oblig·er (one doing a
   favor)
ob·li·gor (one legally
   obligated)
oblit·er·ate
oblit·er·at·ed
oblit·er·a·tion
oblit·er·a·tive
obliv·i·on
obliv·i·ous·ly
ob·lo·quy
ob·nox·ious·ly
ob·scene
ob·scen·i·ty
ob·scur·ant
ob·scu·ran·tism
ob·scu·ran·tist
ob·scu·ra·tion
ob·scure
ob·scured
ob·scure·ly
ob·scure·ness
ob·scu·ri·ty
ob·serv·able
ob·serv·ably
ob·ser·vance
ob·ser·vant
ob·ser·va·tion
ob·serve
ob·served
ob·serv·er
ob·so·les·cence
ob·so·les·cent

75

ob·so·les·cent·ly
ob·so·lete
ob·so·lete·ly
ob·so·lete·ness
ob·stet·ric
ob·stet·ri·cal
ob·ste·tri·cian
ob·sti·na·cy
ob·sti·nate
ob·sti·nate·ly
ob·strep·er·ous
ob·stric·tion
ob·struct
ob·struct·ed
ob·struc·tion·ism
ob·struc·tion·ist
ob·struc·tion·is·tic
ob·struc·tive
ob·struc·tor
ob·vi·ous·ness
oc·ca·sion·al·ly
oc·cip·i·tal
oc·clude
oc·clu·sion
oc·cu·pan·cy
oc·cu·pant
oc·cu·pa·tion·al·ly
oc·cu·pa·tive
oc·cu·pied
oc·cu·pi·er
oc·cu·py·ing
oc·cur
oc·curred
oc·cur·rence
oc·cur·rent
oc·cur·ring

oc·u·list
of·fend·ed
of·fend·er
of·fense
of·fense·less
of·fen·sive·ly
of·fer
of·fered
of·fice
of·fi·cer
of·fi·cial
of·fi·cial·ly
omis·si·ble
omis·sion
omis·sive·ly
omit·ted
omit·ting
om·ni·bus
om·ni·um
oner·ous·ly
oner·ous·ness
on·o·mas·tic adj.
onus pro·ban·di
open·er
open·ly
open·ness
op·er·ate
op·er·at·ed
op·er·a·tion
op·er·a·tion·al
op·er·a·tive
op·er·a·tor
oph·thal·mol·o·gist
opi·ate
opin·ion
opi·um

op·po·nent
op·por·tune
op·por·tun·ism
op·por·tu·ni·ty
op·pos·able
op·posed
op·pos·er
op·po·site
op·po·si·tion
op·pres·sion
op·pres·sive·ly
op·pres·sor
op·ti·cal
op·ti·cian
op·tion
op·tion·al
op·tion·ee
op·tom·e·trist
op·tom·e·try
opus ci·ta·tum
(abbrev.: *op. cit.*)
oral
oral·ly
or·dained
or·dain·er
or·dain·ment
or·deal
or·der
or·der·li·ness
or·der·ly
or·di·nance (law; cf.
ordnance)
or·di·nar·i·ly
or·di·nary
ord·nance (firearms;
cf. *ordinance*)

or·gan·ic
or·gan·i·cal·ly
or·ga·ni·za·tion
or·ga·nize
or·ga·nized
or·ga·niz·er
ori·en·ta·tion
or·i·fice
or·i·gin
orig·i·nal·ly
orig·i·nate
orig·i·nat·ed
orig·i·na·tion
orig·i·na·tive·ly
orig·i·na·tor
or·phan
or·phan·age
or·phaned
or·phan·hood
or·tho·pe·dic
or·tho·pe·dist
os·te·i·tis
os·ten·si·ble
os·ten·si·bly
os·ten·sive
os·ten·sive·ly
os·teo·ar·thri·tis
os·teo·my·eli·tis
os·teo·path·ic
os·teo·path·i·cal·ly
os·te·op·a·thist
os·te·op·a·thy
os·te·ot·o·my
oust·ed
oust·er
out·cast

out·crop
out·er
out·fit·ted
out·fit·ting
out·law
out·lawed
out·rage
out·ra·geous·ly
out·ra·geous·ness
out·right
out·side
out·sid·er
out·spo·ken
out·stand·ing·ly
over·age
over·as·sess·ment
over·awe
over·charge
over·come
over·draft
over·draw
over·drawn
over·drew
over·due
over·haul
over·head
over·is·sue
over·load
over·pow·er
over·pow·ered
over·pow·er·ing·ly
over·priced
over·pride
over·rate
over·rat·ed
over·reached

over·rid·den
over·ride
over·rid·ing
over·rode
over·rule
over·ruled
over·rul·ing
over·seer
overt
over·take
over·tak·en
over·time
over·ture
over·turn
over·wrought
own·er·ship
oy·er and
ter·mi·ner
oyez

pac·i·fi·ca·tion
pa·cif·i·ca·tor
pac·i·fied
pac·i·fist
pac·i·fy
pac·i·fy·ing
pack·aged
pack·ag·er

pac·ta (sing.: *pactum*)
pac·tio
pac·tion·al
pac·tions
pac·tum (pl.: *pacta*)
pal·li·a·tion
pal·lia·tive
pal·pa·ble
pal·pa·bly
pal·pa·tion
pal·pi·ta·tion
pam·phlet
pam·phle·teer
pan·der
pan·dered
pan·der·er
pan·el
pan·eled *or*
  pan·elled
pan·el·ing *or*
  pan·el·ling
para·graph
par·al·lel
par·al·leled
par·al·lel·ing
par·al·lel·ism
pa·ral·y·sis
par·a·lyze
par·a·lyzed
par·a·lyz·ing
par·a·mount
para·noia
para·noi·ac
par·a·noid
par·a·pher·na·lia
para·tit·la

par·celed *or*
  par·celled
par·cel·ing *or*
  par·cel·ling
par·don
par·don·able
par·don·ably
par·doned
par·ent
par·ent·age
pa·ren·tal
par·en·thet·i·cal·ly
pa·ren·ti·cide
pa·re·sis
pa·ri cau·sa
pa·ri de·lic·to
pa·ri·etal
pa·ri ma·te·ria
pa·ri pas·su
par·ish n.
par·i·ty
parked
park·way
par·lia·men·tar·i·an
par·lia·men·ta·ry
pa·ro·chi·al·ism
pa·ro·chi·al·ly
pa·rol (word of mouth)
pa·role (release)
pa·roled
pa·ro·lee
pa·rol·ing
par·ox·ysm
par·ox·ys·mal
par·ri·ci·dal
par·ri·cide

par·tial
par·tial·ly
par·ti·ceps
  cri·mi·nis
par·tic·i·pant
par·tic·i·pate
par·tic·i·pat·ed
par·tic·i·pa·tion
par·tic·i·pa·tive
par·tic·i·pa·tor
par·tic·u·lar
par·tic·u·lar·ize
par·ties
par·ti·tion (division;
  cf. *petition*)
par·ti·tioned
par·ti·tion·er
par·ti·tion·ist
part·ner
part·ner·ship
par·tu·ri·ent
par·tu·ri·tion
par·ty
pas·sage·way
pass·book
pas·sen·ger
pas·sion·ate·ly
pas·sion·less
pas·sive·ly
pas·sive·ness
pas·siv·i·ty
pass·port
pa·tel·la
pa·tent adj.
pat·ent n., v.
pat·ent·abil·i·ty

78

pat·ent·able
pat·ent·ed
pat·en·tee
pa·tent·ly
pa·ter·fa·mil·i·as
pa·ter·nal·ism
pa·ter·nal·ist
pa·ter·nal·is·tic
pa·ter·nal·ly
pa·ter·ni·ty
patho·log·i·cal
pa·thol·o·gist
pa·thol·o·gy
pa·tience
pa·tient
pat·ri·ci·dal
pat·ri·cide
pat·ri·mo·ni·al
pat·ri·mo·ni·um
pat·ri·mo·ny
pa·trol
pa·trolled
pa·trol·ler
pa·trol·ling
pa·trol·man
pa·tron
pa·tron·age
pa·tron·ess fem.
pa·tron·ize
pau·per
pau·per·ism
pau·per·ize
pawn
pawn·bro·ker
pawned
pawn·ee

pawn·er *or*
  paw·nor
pay·able
pay·ee
pay·er *or*
  pay·or
pay·mas·ter
pay·ment
peace·able·ness
peace·ably
pec·u·late
pec·u·la·tion
pec·u·la·tor
pe·cu·lia pl.
pe·cu·liar
pe·cu·liar·i·ty
pe·cu·liar·ly
pe·cu·li·um sing.
pe·cu·ni·ary
ped·dled
ped·dler
ped·dling
pe·des·tri·an
pe·di·a·tri·cian
pe·di·at·rics
ped·i·gree
ped·i·greed
pel·vis
pe·nal
pe·nal·iza·tion
pe·nal·ize
pe·nal·ized
pe·nal·ly
pen·al·ty
pen·den·cy
pen·dens

pen·dent *or*
  pen·dant
pen·den·te lite
pen·i·ten·tia·ry
pen·sion
pen·sioned
pen·sion·er
per an·num
per cap·i·ta
per·ceiv·able
per·ceive
per·cent
per·cent·age
per·cen·tile
per cen·tum
per con·tra
per cu·ri·am
per di·em
per·dur·able
per·du·ra·bly
pe·remp·tion
pe·remp·to·ri·ly
pe·remp·to·ri·ness
pe·remp·to·ry
pe·ren·ni·al·ly
per·fect
per·fect·ed
per·fect·er n.
per·fect·ibil·i·ty
per·fect·ible
per·fec·tion
per·fec·tive·ly
per·fec·tive·ness
per·fect·ly
per·fect·ness
per·fid·i·ous·ly

per·fid·i·ous·ness
per·fi·dy
per·form·able
per·for·mance
per·formed
per·form·er
per·il·ous·ly
per·il·ous·ness
pe·ri·od·ic
pe·ri·od·i·cal·ly
pe·riph·er·al
pe·riph·ery
per·ish v.
per·ish·abil·i·ty
per·ish·able
per·ished
peri·to·ni·tis
per·jure
per·jured
per·jur·er
per·jur·ing
per·ju·ry
per·ma·nence
per·ma·nen·cy
per·ma·nent·ly
per·ma·nent·ness
per·mis·si·ble
per·mis·si·ble·ness
per·mis·si·bly
per·mis·sion
per·mis·sive
per·mis·sive·ly
per·mis·sive·ness
per·mit
per·mit·ted
per·mit·tee

per·mit·ter
per·mit·ting
per·mu·ta·tion
per·nan·cy
per·pe·trate
per·pe·trat·ed
per·pe·tra·tion
per·pe·tra·tor
per·pet·u·al·ly
per·pet·u·ate
per·pet·u·at·ed
per·pet·u·a·tion
per·pet·u·a·tor
per·pe·tu·it·ies
per·pe·tu·ity
per·qui·site
per se
per·so·na
per·son·al
per·son·al·i·ty
per·son·al·ize
per·son·al·ly
per·son·al·ty
per·son·ate
per·son·ation
per·son·a·tor
per stir·pes
per·suade
per·suad·ed
per·suad·er
per·sua·sion
per·sua·sive
per·sua·sive·ly
per·sua·sive·ness
per·tain
per·tained

per·ti·nen·cy
per·ti·nent
per·verse
per·verse·ly
per·verse·ness
per·ver·sion
per·ver·si·ty
per·ver·sive
per·vert
per·vert·ed
per·vert·er
pe·tit
pe·ti·tion (request; cf.
    partition)
pe·ti·tion·ary
pe·ti·tioned
pe·ti·tion·ee
pe·ti·tion·er
pe·tro·le·um
pet·ty
pha·lanx sing.
pha·lanx·es *or*
    pha·lan·ges pl.
phar·ma·cist
phar·ma·cy
pho·to·copy
pho·to·graph
pho·to·graphed
pho·tog·ra·pher
pho·to·graph·ic
pho·to·graph·i·cal·ly
pho·tog·ra·phy
pho·to·stat·ic
phrase·ol·o·gy
phys·i·cal (bodily; cf.
    fiscal)

80

phys·i·cal·ly
phy·si·cian
phys·io·ther·a·py
pick·et
pick·et·ed
pick·et·er
pick·et·ing
pick·pock·et
pig·nus
pil·fer
pil·fer·age
pil·fered
pil·fer·er
pil·lage
pil·laged
pil·lag·er
pi·lot
pi·lot·age
pi·lot·ed
pi·ra·cy
pi·rate
pi·rat·i·cal·ly
pis·tol
piti·ful·ly
piti·ful·ness
pit·tance
plac·ard
plac·er
plac·i·tum
pla·gia·rism
pla·gia·rist
pla·gia·ris·tic
pla·gia·rize
pla·gia·rized
plain·tiff
plain·tiffs

plat
plau·si·bil·i·ty
plau·si·ble
plau·si·bly
plea
plead
plead·ed
plead·er
pleb·i·scite
pledge
pledged
pledg·ee
pledg·er *or*
  pled·gor
pledg·ing
ple·na·ry
pleni·po·ten·tia·ry
pleu·ra
pleu·ral
pleu·ri·sy
plot·ted
plot·ting
plun·der
plun·der·able
plun·dered
plun·der·er
plu·ral
plu·ral·i·ty
plu·ral·ly
pneu·mo·nia
poach
poached
poach·er
poi·son
poi·soned
poi·son·ous·ly

po·lice
po·liced
po·lice·man
pol·i·cy
pol·i·cy·hold·er
pol·i·tic adj.
po·lit·i·cal
pol·i·ti·cian
pol·i·tick v.
pol·i·tics n.
poll tax
pol·lu·tant
pol·lute
pol·lut·ed
pol·lut·er
pol·lut·ing
pol·lu·tion
poly·an·dry
po·lyg·a·mous
po·lyg·a·my
pop·u·lace n.
pop·u·lous adj.
por·nog·ra·pher
por·no·graph·ic
por·no·graph·i·cal·ly
por·nog·ra·phy
port·fo·lio
pos·i·tive
pos·i·tiv·ist
pos·sess
pos·sessed
pos·sess·es
pos·sess·ing
pos·ses·sion
pos·ses·sive·ly
pos·ses·sive·ness

pos·ses·sor
pos·ses·so·ry
pos·si·bil·i·ty
pos·si·ble
pos·si·bly
post·age
post·al
post·date
post·dat·ed
pos·ter·i·ty
post hoc
post·hu·mous·ly
post·hu·mous·ness
post·mar·i·tal
post·mark
post·mas·ter
post·mor·tem adj.
post—mor·tem adv.
post·nat·al
post·na·tal·ly
post·nup·tial
post·nup·tial·ly
post—obit
post of·fice
post·pon·able
post·pone
post·poned
post·pone·ment
post·pon·er
po·ta·ble
po·tent
po·ten·tial
po·ten·ti·al·i·ty
po·ten·tial·ly
po·ten·ti·ate
pow·er·less·ly

pow·er·less·ness
pow·er of
    at·tor·ney
prac·ti·ca·bil·i·ty
prac·ti·ca·ble
prac·ti·cal·i·ty
prac·ti·cal·ly
prac·tice
prac·ticed
prac·ti·tion·er
prae·ci·pe
    or pre·ci·pe
prae·ci·pe in
    cap·i·te
prae·dia pl.
prae·di·um sing.
pray (beseech; cf.
    prey)
prayed
prayer (request)
pray·er (requester)
pre·am·ble
pre·ap·point·ed
pre·car·i·ous·ly
pre·car·i·ous·ness
prec·a·to·ry
pre·cau·tion·ary
pre·cede
pre·ce·dence
pre·ce·dent adj.
prec·e·dent n.
pre·cept
pre·cinct
pre·cip·i·tance
pre·cip·i·tan·cy
pre·cip·i·tant·ly

pre·cip·i·tate
pre·cip·i·tat·ed
pre·cip·i·ta·tion
pre·cise·ly
pre·cise·ness
pre·clude
pre·clud·ed
pre·clu·sion
pre·clu·sive·ly
pre·con·tract
pre·de·cease
pre·de·ceased
pre·de·ces·sor
pre·de·ter·mi·na·
    tion
pre·de·ter·mined
pred·i·cate
pred·i·cat·ed
pred·i·ca·tion
pred·i·ca·tive
pre·dom·i·nance
pre·dom·i·nan·cy
pre·dom·i·nant·ly
pre·dom·i·nate·ly
pre·empt
pre·empt·ed
pre·emp·tion
pre·emp·tive·ly
pre·emp·tor
pre·ex·am·i·na·tion
pre·fer
pref·er·a·bil·i·ty
pref·er·a·ble
pref·er·a·bly
pref·er·ence
pref·er·en·tial·ly

pre·ferred
pre·fer·ring
preg·na·bil·i·ty
preg·nan·cy
preg·nant·ly
prej·u·dice
prej·u·diced
prej·u·di·cial
prej·u·di·cial·ly
prej·u·di·cial·ness
prej·u·dic·ing
pre·lim·i·nary
pre·med·i·tat·ed·ly
pre·med·i·ta·tion
pre·med·i·ta·tive
pre·med·i·ta·tor
prem·ise
prem·is·es
pre·mi·um
prep·a·ra·tion
pre·pa·ra·to·ry
pre·pon·der·ance
pre·pon·der·an·cy
pre·pon·der·ant·ly
pre·pon·der·a·tion
pre·rog·a·tive
pre·rog·a·tived adj.
pre·scrib·able
pre·scribe
pre·scribed
pre·scrip·ti·ble
pre·scrip·tion
pres·ence
pre·sent v.
pres·ent n., adj.
pre·sen·ta·tion

pre·sent·ed
pre·sen·tee
pre·sent·er
pres·ent·ly
pre·sent·ment
pres·er·va·tion
pre·serve
pre·served
pre·serv·er
pre·side
pre·sid·ed
pres·i·den·cy
pres·i·dent
pres·i·den·tial
pre·sid·ing
pre·sum·ably
pre·sume
pre·sumed
pre·sum·er
pre·sum·ing·ly
pre·sump·tion
pre·sump·tive·ly
pre·sump·tu·ous·ly
pre·sup·pose
pre·sup·po·si·tion
pre·tend·ed·ly
pre·tend·er
pre·tense or
    pre·tence
pre·tensed adj.
pre·tens·es
pre·ten·sion
pre·ten·tious·ly
pre·ten·tious·ness
pre·ter·mit
pre·ter·mit·ted

pre·ter·mit·ting
pre·text
pre·tri·al
pre·tried
pre·vail
prev·a·lence
prev·a·lent
pre·var·i·cate
pre·var·i·cat·ed
pre·var·i·cat·ing
pre·var·i·ca·tion
pre·var·i·ca·tor
pre·vent
pre·vent·abil·i·ty
pre·vent·able
pre·ven·ta·tive
pre·vent·ed
pre·vent·er
pre·ven·tion
pre·ven·tive·ly
pre·vi·ous·ly
pre·vi·ous·ness
prey (victim; cf. pray)
pri·ma fa·cie
pri·mage
pri·ma·ry
pri·mo·gen·i·tor
pri·mo·gen·i·ture
prin·ci·pal (chief; cf.
    principle)
prin·ci·pal·ly
prin·ci·ple (rule; cf.
    principal)
prin·ci·pled
pri·or
pri·or·i·ty

83

pris·on
pris·on·er
pri·va·cy
pri·vate·ly
pri·vate·ness
pri·va·tion
priv·i·lege
priv·i·leged
priv·i·ty
privy adj., n.
prob·a·bil·i·ty
prob·a·ble
prob·a·bly
pro·bate
pro·bat·ed
pro·ba·tion
pro·ba·tion·al
pro·ba·tion·ary
pro·ba·tion·er
pro·ba·tive
probe
probed
prob·ing
pro bo·no
   pub·li·co
pro·ce·dur·al
pro·ce·dur·al·ly
pro·ce·dure
pro·ceed v.
pro·ceed·ed
pro·ceed·ing
pro·ceeds n., v.
pro·cess
pro·cessed
pro·cess·es
pro·cess·ing

pro·ces·sor
pro·chein ami
   or pro·chein
      amy
pro·claim
pro·claimed
pro·claim·er
proc·la·ma·tion
pro con·fes·so
pro·cre·ate
pro·cre·ation
pro·cre·ative
pro·cre·ator
proc·tor
proc·to·ri·al
proc·u·ra·tion
proc·u·ra·tor
proc·u·ra·to·ri·al
pro·cure
pro·cured
pro·cure·ment
pro·cur·er
pro·cur·ing
pro·di·tion
prod·i·tor
pro·duce
pro·duced
pro·duc·er
prod·uct
pro·duc·tion
pro·duc·tion·al
pro·fane
pro·fane·ly
pro·fane·ness
pro·fan·i·ty
pro·fess

pro·fessed
pro·fess·ing
pro·fes·sion
pro·fes·sion·al·ly
pro·file
prof·it
prof·it·abil·i·ty
prof·it·able·ness
prof·it·ed
prof·i·teer
pro for·ma
pro·gen·i·tor
prog·e·ny
prog·no·sis
prog·nos·tic
prog·ress n.
pro·gress v.
pro·gressed
pro·gres·sion
pro·gres·sion·al
pro·hib·it
pro·hib·it·ed
pro·hi·bi·tion
pro·hib·i·tive
pro·lapse
pro·le·tar·i·an
pro·le·tar·i·at
pro·li·cid·al
pro·li·cide
pro·lix
pro·lix·i·ty
pro·lix·ly
pro·long
pro·lon·gate
pro·lon·ga·tion
pro·longed

pro·mis·cu·ity
pro·mis·cu·ous
pro·mis·cu·ous·ly
prom·ise
prom·ised
prom·is·ee
prom·is·er
prom·i·sor
prom·is·sory
pro·mote
pro·mot·ed
pro·mot·er
pro·mo·tion·al
prompt·ed
prompt·er
prompt·ly
pro·mul·gate
pro·mul·gat·ed
pro·mul·ga·tion
pro·mul·ga·tor
proof
prop·a·gate
prop·a·ga·tion
prop·a·ga·tor
prop·er·ly
prop·er·ty
pro·pin·qui·ty
pro·po·nent
pro·por·tion·ate·ly
pro·pos·al
pro·pose
pro·posed
pro·pos·er
prop·o·si·tion
prop·o·si·tion·al
pro·pound·ed

pro·pound·er
pro·pri·etary
pro·pri·etor
pro·pri·etor·ship
pro·pri·etress fem.
pro·pri·ety
prop·ter
  de·fec·tum
  san·gui·nis
prop·ter
  de·lic·tum
prop·ter hoc
pro ra·ta
pro·rate
pro·rat·ed
pro·rogue
pro·rogued
pro·scribe
pro·scrib·er
pros·e·cute
pros·e·cut·ed
pros·e·cut·ing
pros·e·cu·tion
pros·e·cu·tor
pros·pect
pro·spec·tive
pro·spec·tive·ly
pro·spec·tus
pros·per·ous
pros·the·sis
pros·thet·ic
pros·ti·tute
pros·ti·tut·ed
pros·ti·tu·tion
pro tan·to
pro·tect·ed

pro·tec·tion
pro·tec·tive
pro·tec·tor
pro tem
pro tem·po·re
pro·tes·ta·tion
pro·test·ed
pro·tho·no·tar·i·al
pro·tho·no·ta·ry
pro·to·col
prov·able
prov·ably
pro·vide
pro·vid·ed
pro·vid·er
pro·vi·sion
pro·vi·sion·al
pro·vi·so
pro·vi·so·ry
prov·o·ca·tion
pro·voc·a·tive
pro·voke
pro·voked
pro·vok·ing·ly
pro·vost
prox·ies
prox·i·mate
prox·i·mate·ly
prox·im·i·ty
proxy
pru·dence
pru·dent
pru·dent·ly
pseu·do·sci·en·tif·ic
psy·chi·at·ric
psy·chi·a·trist

psy·chi·a·try
psy·cho·an·a·lyst
psy·cho·an·a·lyt·i-
cal
psy·cho·an·a·lyze
psy·cho·log·i·cal
psy·cho·log·i·cal·ly
psy·chol·o·gist
psy·chol·o·gy
psy·cho·neu·ro·sis
psy·cho·neu·rot·ic
psy·cho·path·ic
psy·cho·path·i·cal·ly
psy·chop·a·thy
psy·cho·ses pl.
psy·cho·sis sing.
psy·cho·so·ma·tic
psy·cho·ther·a·pist
psy·cho·ther·a·py
pu·ber·ty
pu·bic
pub·li·ca·tion
pu·bli·ci ju·ris
pub·lic·i·ty
pub·lic·ly
pub·lic·ness
pub·lish·able
pub·lished
pub·lish·er
pu·er·ile
pu·er·il·i·ty
puff·er
pu·gi·list
pul·mo·nary
pun·ish·abil·i·ty
pun·ish·able

pun·ished
pun·ish·er
pun·ish·ment
pu·ni·tive
pu·ni·tive·ly
pu·ni·tive·ness
pur au·tre vie
pur·ga·tion
pur·ga·to·ry
purge
purged
purg·er
pur·loin
pur·loin·er
pur·part
pur·par·ty
pur·port·ed
pur·pose
pur·pose·ly
pur·pres·ture
purs·er
pur·su·al
pur·su·ance
pur·su·ant
pur·sue
pur·sued
pur·su·er
pur·su·ing
pur·suit
pu·ru·lent
pur·view
pu·ta·tive
pu·ta·tive·ly
py·ro·ma·nia
py·ro·ma·ni·ac
py·ro·ma·ni·a·cal

qua
quad·rant
qua·dran·tal
qua·droon
qual·i·fi·ca·tion
qual·i·fied
qual·i·fied·ly
qual·i·fi·er
qual·i·fy·ing
qual·i·ty
quan·ta pl.
quan·ti mi·nor·is
quan·tum sing.
quan·tum me·ru·it
quan·tum
va·le·bant
quar·ant·ine
quar·rel
quar·reled
  or quar·relled
quar·rel·ing
  or quar·rel·ling
quar·ter·ly
quash
quashed
qua·si con·tract
qua·si in rem
quay
quay·age

86

ques·tion·able·ness
ques·tion·ably
ques·tioned
quib·ble
quib·bled
quib·bling
quid pro quo
quit·claim
quit·tance
quo
quo·ad hoc
quo an·i·mo
quod com·pu·tet
quod no·ta
quod vi·de
   (abbrev.: *q.v.*)
quo ju·re
quo·rum
quo·ta
quot·able
quo·ta·tion
quot·ed
quo war·ran·to
q.v. (abbreviation of
   quod vide)

R

rac·ism
rac·ist

rack·et
rack·e·teer
rad·i·cal
ra·di·ol·o·gist
ra·di·ol·o·gy
ra·di·us
rail·road
ran·som
ran·somed
ran·som·er
rape
rap·er
rap·ine
rap·ing
rap·ist
rat·able *or*
   rate·able
rat·i·fi·ca·tion
rat·i·fied
rat·i·fy
rat·i·fy·ing
ra·tio de·ci·den·di
ra·tio le·gis
ra·tio·nal adj.
ra·tio·nale n.
ra·tio·nal·i·ty
ra·tio·nal·iza·tion
ra·tio·nal·ly
ra·ti·o·ne
   do·mi·ci·lii
ra·ti·o·ne
   ma·te·ri·ae
ra·ti·o·ne
   per·son·ae
rav·age
rav·aged

rav·ish
rav·ished
rav·ish·er
rav·ish·ment
re·ad·just·ment
re·af·firm
re·af·fir·ma·tion
re·al·is·tic
re·al·is·ti·cal·ly
re·al·i·ty
re·al·iz·able
re·al·iza·tion
re·al·le·ga·tion
re·al·lege
re·al·lo·cate
re·al·lo·ca·tion
re·al·lot·ment
re·al·ty
re·ap·por·tioned
re·ap·por·tion·ing
re·ap·por·tion·ment
re·ap·prais·al
re·ar·gu·ment
rea·son·able·ness
rea·son·ably
re·as·sess·ment
re·as·sur·ance
re·bate
reb·el n., adj.
re·bel v.
re·belled
re·bel·ling
re·bel·lion
re·bel·lious·ness
re·but·ta·ble
re·but·tal

87

re·but·ted
re·but·ter
re·but·ting
re·cal·ci·trant
re·call
re·cant
re·cant·ed
re·ca·pit·u·late
re·cap·ture
re·cede
re·ced·ed
re·ceipt
re·ceipt·or
re·ceiv·able
re·ceive
re·ceiv·er
re·ceiv·er·ship
re·cep·tive·ly
re·cep·tiv·i·ty
re·cess
re·cessed
re·cess·ing
re·ces·sion
re·cid·i·vist
re·cip·i·ent
re·cip·ro·cal
re·cip·ro·cate
re·cip·ro·cat·ed
re·cip·ro·ca·tion
rec·i·proc·i·ty
re·ci·sion
re·cit·al
reck·less·ly
reck·less·ness
reck·on
reck·oned

re·claim·able
re·claimed
rec·la·ma·tion
rec·og·ni·tion
rec·og·niz·able
rec·og·niz·ably
re·cog·ni·zance
rec·og·nize
rec·og·nized
re·cog·ni·zee
re·cog·ni·zor
re—col·lect (collect again)
rec·ol·lect (recall)
rec·ol·lec·tion
rec·om·mend
rec·om·men·da·tion
rec·om·mend·ed
rec·om·pense
rec·om·pen·sive
re·com·pu·ta·tion
re·com·pute
re·com·put·ed
rec·on·cil·abil·i·ty
rec·on·cil·able
rec·on·cile
rec·on·ciled
rec·on·cil·i·a·tion
rec·on·cil·ia·to·ry
re·con·di·tioned
re·con·firm
re·con·fir·ma·tion
re·con·nais·sance
re·con·noi·ter
re·con·sid·er
re·con·sid·er·a·tion

re·con·sign·ment
re·con·sol·i·da·tion
re·con·struct
re·con·struct·ed
re·con·struc·tion
re·con·struc·tive
re·con·tin·u·ance
re·con·ver·sion
re·con·vey·ance
re·con·veyed
rec·ord n., adj.
re·cord v.
re·cord·are
re·cord·ed
re·cord·er
re·coup
re·coup·able
re·couped
re·coup·ment
re·course
re·cov·er·able
re·cov·ered
re·cov·er·ee
re·cov·er·er
re·cov·er·or
re·cov·ery
re·crim·i·nate
re·crim·i·na·tion
re·crim·i·na·tor
re·crim·i·na·to·ry
rec·ti·fi·able
rec·ti·fi·ca·tion
rec·ti·fied
rec·ti·fy
rec·ti·fy·ing
re·cu·per·ate

re·cur
re·curred
re·cur·rence
re·cur·rent
re·cur·ring
rec·u·sa·tion
re·cu·sa·tor
re·cuse
red·den·dum
red·di·tion
re·deem
re·deem·able
re·deemed
re·de·liv·ery
re·demp·tion
re·de·ter·mi·na·tion
red·hi·bi·tion
re·di·rect
re·di·rec·tion
re·dis·tri·bute
re·dis·tri·bu·tion
re·draft
re·dress
re·dress·er
re·duc·tio ad
  ab·sur·dum
re·duc·tion
re·dun·dan·cy
re·dun·dant
re·elect
re·elec·tion
re·en·act
re·en·act·ed
re·en·act·ment
re·en·try
re·ex·am·i·na·tion

re·ex·am·ine
re·ex·am·ined
re·fer
ref·er·ee
ref·er·eed
ref·er·ee·ing
ref·er·ence
ref·er·en·dum
re·fer·ral
re·ferred
re·fer·ring
re·fi·nanc·ing
re·flect·ed
re·flec·tion
ref·or·ma·tion
re·for·ma·to·ry
re·formed
re·form·er
re·frac·to·ry
ref·uge (sanctuary)
ref·u·gee (seeker of
  refuge)
re·fund·able
re·fund·ed
re·fus·al
re·fuse v.
ref·use n., adj.
re·fus·er
re·fut·able
ref·u·ta·tion
re·fute
re·fut·ed
re·fut·er
re·gion·al
reg·is·ter
reg·is·tered

reg·is·trant
reg·is·trar
reg·is·tra·tion
reg·is·try
re·gress
re·gressed
re·gres·sion
re·gres·sive·ly
re·gres·sive·ness
re·gret·ta·ble
re·gret·ted
re·gret·ting
reg·u·lar·ly
reg·u·late
reg·u·lat·ed
reg·u·la·tion
reg·u·la·tive
reg·u·la·tor
reg·u·la·to·ry
re·ha·bil·i·tate
re·ha·bil·i·tat·ed
re·ha·bil·i·ta·tion
re·hear·ing
re·im·burs·able
re·im·burse
re·im·bursed
re·im·burse·ment
re·in·state
re·in·stat·ed
re·in·state·ment
re·in·sure
re·in·vest·ment
re·is·sue
re·it·er·ate
re·it·er·at·ed
re·it·er·a·tion

re·ject·ed
re·ject·ee
re·ject·er *or*
 re·ject·or
re·jec·tion
re·jec·tive
re·join
re·join·der
re·judge
re·lat·ed
re·la·tion·ship
rel·a·tive·ness
re·lease
re·leased
re·leas·es
re·lea·sor *or*
 re·leas·er
re·lent·less·ly
rel·e·vance
rel·e·van·cy
rel·e·vant
re·li·abil·i·ty
re·li·able
re·li·ance
re·li·ant
rel·ict
re·lied
re·lief
re·lieve
re·lieved
re·lin·quish
re·lin·quished
re·lin·quish·ment
re·luc·tance
re·luc·tant
re·ly·ing

rem
re·main·der
re·main·der·man
re·mand·ed
re·mand·ing
re·ma·nent
re·mar·riage
re·mar·ried
re·mar·ry
re·me·di·a·ble
re·me·di·a·bly
re·me·di·al
re·me·di·al·ly
rem·e·died
rem·e·dies
rem·e·di·less
rem·e·dy
rem·e·dy·ing
re·mise v.
re·miss adj.
re·mis·si·bly
re·mis·sion
re·mis·sive
re·mit
re·mit·tance
re·mit·ted
re·mit·tee
re·mit·ter
re·mit·ti·tur
 dam·na
re·mon·strance
re·mon·strate
re·mon·strat·ed
re·mon·stra·tive
re·morse·ful
re·morse·less

re·mote·ness
re·mov·able
re·mov·al
re·moved
re·mov·er
re·mu·ner·ate
re·mu·ner·a·tion
re·mu·ner·a·tive·ly
re·mu·ner·a·tive·ness
ren·der
ren·der·er
ren·dez·vous
re·nege
re·neged
re·neg·ing
re·ne·go·tia·ble
re·ne·go·ti·ate
re·ne·go·ti·at·ed
re·ne·go·ti·a·tion
re·new·able
re·new·al
re·newed
re·nounce
re·nounced
re·nounce·ment
re·nounc·ing
ren·o·vate
ren·o·vat·ed
ren·o·va·tion
rent·al
rent·ed
rent·er
re·nun·ci·a·tion
re·or·ga·ni·za·tion
rep·a·ra·tion
re·pa·tri·ate

re·pa·tri·at·ed
re·pa·tri·a·tion
re·pay·ment
re·pealed
re·peal·er
re·peat·ed
re·peat·er
re·pel
re·pelled
re·pel·ling
re·pen·tant
re·pent·ed
re·per·cus·sion
rep·e·ti·tion
rep·e·ti·tious
re·place·able
re·place·ment
re·plead
re·plead·er
re·plevi·able
re·plev·ied
re·plev·in
re·plevy
re·plevy·ing
re·pli·ant
rep·li·ca·tion
re·port·ed·ly
re·pos·i·to·ry
re·pos·sess
re·pos·sessed
re·pos·sess·ing
re·pos·ses·sion
rep·re·hen·si·ble
rep·re·hen·sion
re—pre·sent (present
    again)

rep·re·sent (take
    the place of)
rep·re·sent·able
rep·re·sen·ta·tion
rep·re·sen·ta·tive
rep·re·sent·ed
re·press
re·pressed
re·press·ing
re·pres·sion
re·pres·sive
re·pres·sor
re·priev·al
re·prieve
rep·ri·mand
rep·ri·mand·ed
re·pri·sal
re·prise
re·proach
rep·ro·bate
rep·ro·ba·tion
re·pub·lic
re·pub·li·can
re·pub·li·ca·tion
re·pu·di·ate
re·pu·di·at·ed
re·pu·di·a·tion
re·pu·di·a·tor
re·pugn
re·pug·nance
re·pug·nant
rep·u·ta·ble
rep·u·ta·bly
rep·u·ta·tion
re·pute
re·put·ed·ly

re·quest·ed
re·quest·er
re·quire
re·quired
re·quire·ment
req·ui·site
req·ui·si·tion·ing
re·quit·al
re·reg·is·tered
re·sale
re·scind
re·scind·ed
re·scind·er
re·scind·ing
re·scis·sion
re·sec·tion
re·sem·blance
re·sem·ble
re·sem·bled
re·sem·bling
res·er·va·tion
re·serve
re·set·tle·ment
res ges·tae
re·side
re·sid·ed
res·i·dence
res·i·dent
res·i·den·tial
re·sid·u·al
re·sid·u·al·ly
re·sid·u·ary
res·i·due
re·sid·u·um
re·sign
res·ig·na·tion

re·sign·ed·ly
re·sign·ee
re·sign·er
res in·ter ali·os ac·ta
res ip·sa lo·qui·tur
re·sist
re·sis·tance
re·sis·tant
re·sist·ed
res ju·di·ca·ta
res mo·bi·les
res no·va
res·o·lute
res·o·lu·tion
re·solv·able
re·solve
re·solved
re·spect·abil·i·ty
re·spect·able
re·spect·ful·ly
re·spec·tive
re·spec·tive·ly
re·spite
re·spond
re·spon·de·at su·pe·ri·or
re·spond·ed
re·spon·dent
re·spond·er
re·spon·si·bil·i·ty
re·spon·si·ble
re·spon·si·ble·ness
re·spon·si·bly
re·spon·sive

res·ti·tu·tion
res·to·ra·tion
re·stor·ative
re·store
re·strain·able
re·strained
re·strain·ed·ly
re·strain·er
re·straint
re·strict·ed
re·stric·tion
re·stric·tive·ly
re·stric·tive·ness
re·sul·tant
re·sult·ed
re·sume v.
ré·su·mé (summary)
re·sumed
re·sum·mons
re·sump·tion
re·tail·er
re·tain·age
re·tained
re·tain·er
re·tal·i·ate
re·tal·i·at·ed
re·tal·i·a·tion
re·tal·ia·to·ry
re·ten·tion
re·ten·tive·ly
re·ten·tive·ness
ret·i·na
ret·i·nal
re·tire·ment
re·tort
re·tort·ed

re·tor·tion
re·tract
re·tract·ed
re·trac·tion
re·trax·it
re·tri·al
ret·ri·bu·tion
re·trib·u·tive·ly
re·trib·u·to·ry
re·tro·ac·tion
re·tro·ac·tive
re·tro·ac·tive·ly
re·tro·ac·tiv·i·ty
re·tro·cede
re·tro·ces·sion
re·tro·spect
re·tro·spec·tive
re·turn·able
re·turned
re·val·i·date
re·val·i·da·tion
re·val·u·ate
re·val·u·a·tion
re·ven·di·cate
re·ven·di·ca·tion
re·venge·ful
rev·e·nue
rev·e·nu·er
re·vcr·sal
re·verse
re·versed
re·verse·ly
re·vers·ible
re·ver·sion·ary
re·ver·sion·er
re·vert

re·vert·ed
re·vert·er
re·vest
re·vi·sion·ary
re·vi·so·ry
re·viv·al
re·vi·ver
re·vo·ca·ble
re·vo·ca·tion
re·vok·able
re·voke
re·voked
rev·o·lu·tion
rev·o·lu·tion·ary
rev·o·lu·tion·ist
re·volved
re·volv·er
re·ward·ed
re·zoned
rid·er
ri·fle
ri·fled
ri·fling
right·ful·ly
rig·or mor·tis
ri·ot·ed
ri·ot·er
ri·ot·ous·ly
ri·ot·ous·ness
ri·par·i·an
robbed
rob·ber
rob·bery
rob·bing
roent·gen·o·grams
roent·gen·ol·o·gist

roent·gen·ol·o·gy
rog·a·to·ry
Ror·schach
ros·ter
ru·in·ous
ruled
rul·ing
ru·mor
ru·mored
ru·ral

sab·o·tage
sab·o·teur
sac·ri·fice
sac·ri·ficed
sac·ri·lege
sac·ri·le·gious·ly
sac·ri·le·gious·ness
sa·cro·il·i·ac
sa·crum
sa·dism
sa·dist
sa·dis·tic
sa·dis·ti·cal·ly
safe—de·pos·it adj.
safe·guard
safe·ly
safe·ty

sal·abil·i·ty
sal·able or
  sale·able
sal·a·ry
sal·u·tary
sal·vage·able
sal·vaged
sal·vag·er
sa·nae men·tis
san·a·to·ri·um
sanc·tion
sanc·tioned
sanc·tu·ary
sane
san·er
san·est
san·gui·nary
san·i·tar·i·um
san·i·tary
san·i·ta·tion
san·i·ty
sans re·cours
sa·nus
sat·is·fac·tion
sat·is·fac·to·ri·ly
sat·is·fac·to·ry
sat·is·fied
sat·is·fy·ing
sav·age·ly
sav·age·ry
say—so n.
scaf·fold
scan·dal
scan·dal·iza·tion
scan·dal·ize
scan·dal·ized

scan·dal·iz·er
scan·dal·ous
scan·dal·ous·ly
scan·dal·ous·ness
scape·goat
scap·u·la
scarce
scar·ci·ty
scathed
scath·ing
sched·ule
sched·uled
scheme
schemed
schem·er
schem·ing
schism
schiz·o·phre·nia
schiz·o·phre·nic
sci·en·ter
sci·en·tif·ic
sci·li·cet (abbrev.: *ss.* or *s.*)
scin·til·la ju·ris
sci·re fa·cias
sci·re fe·ci
scle·ro·sis
scope
scrawl
scrip·tum
scroll
scru·pu·lous·ly
scru·ti·ny
scuf·fle
scuf·fling
scur·ri·lous

sealed
sea·man
searched
sea·wor·thi·ness
sea·wor·thy
se·clude
se·clud·ed
se·clu·sion
sec·ond
sec·ond·ar·i·ly
sec·ond·ary
se·cre·cy
se·cret n., adj.
sec·re·tary
se·crete v.
se·cre·tive·ly
se·cret·ly
sec·tar·i·an
sec·tion·al·ism
sec·tion·al·ly
sec·u·lar
se·cun·dum al·le·ga·ta et pro·ba·ta
se·cun·dum bo·nos mo·res
se·cun·dum le·gem
se·cur·ance
se·cure
se·cure·ment
se·cure·ness
se·cu·ri·ties
se·cu·ri·ty
sed·a·tive

se·di·tion
se·di·tion·ary
se·di·tious·ly
se·di·tious·ness
se·duced
se·duc·er
se·duc·ing
se·duc·tion
se·duc·tive·ness
se·duc·tress fem.
sed·u·lous·ly
seg·re·gate
seg·re·gat·ed
seg·re·ga·tion
sei·sin
seized
seiz·ing
sei·zor
sei·zure
se·lect·men
self—con·fes·sion
self—de·fense
self—ex·e·cut·ing
self—in·crim·i·na·tion
self—pres·er·va·tion
self—pro·tec·tion
self—sup·port
sell·er (one who sells; cf. *cellar*)
sell·out n.
sell out v.
semi·an·nu·al·ly
sem·per pa·ra·tus
sen·ate

94

sen·a·tor
sen·a·to·ri·al
se·nile
se·nile·ly
se·nil·i·ty
se·nior
se·nior·i·ty
sen·sa·tion·al
sens·es (feelings; cf. *census*)
sen·si·bil·i·ty
sen·si·ble
sen·si·bly
sen·si·tive
sen·si·tiv·i·ty
sen·tence
sen·tenced
sen·tenc·ing
sen·ti·ment
sen·ti·nel
sep·a·ra·bil·i·ty
sep·a·rate·ly
sep·a·rate·ness
sep·ar·a·tion
se·quel
se·que·la
se·ques·ter
se·que·stra·tion
se·que·stra·tor
se·qui·tur
se·ri·al·ly
se·ri·ate·ly
se·ri·a·tim
ser·vant
serv·er
ser·vice

ser·vice·able
ser·vice·man
ser·vi·ent
ser·vile
ser·vil·i·ty
ser·vi·tude
ses·sion (meeting; cf. *cession*)
ses·sion·al
ses·sion·ary
set·tle
set·tled
set·tle·ment
set·tler (pioneer)
set·tling
set·tlor (maker)
sev·er·abil·i·ty
sev·er·able
sev·er·al
sev·er·al·ly
sev·er·al·ty
sev·er·ance
sev·ered
se·vere·ly
sev·er·ing
se·ver·i·ty
sex·u·al·ly
shad·owed
shad·ow·ing
sham
shammed
sham·ming
shang·hai
shang·haied
shang·hai·ing
share·hold·er

shar·er
shel·ter
shel·tered
sher·iff
ship·per
ship·ping
shop·lift·er
shop·lift·ing
shop right
short·sight·ed·ness
short—term·er
short—tim·er
shot·gun
shriev·al·ty
shrink·age
sib·ling
sic
sight (vision; cf. *cite, site*)
sight draft
sig·il
sig·il·lum
sig·nal
sig·na·to·ry
sig·na·ture
signed
sign·er
sig·nif·i·cance
sig·nif·i·cant·ly
sig·ni·fi·ca·tion
sig·ni·fied
sig·ni·fy
sig·ni·fy·ing
si·lence
si·lenced
si·lenc·er

si·lent
sim·i·lar·i·ty
sim·i·lar·ly
sim·ple
sim·plex
  ob·li·ga·to
sim·u·late
sim·u·lat·ed
sim·u·la·tion
sim·u·la·tor
si·mul·ta·neous
si·mul·ta·neous·ly
sin·cere·ly
sin·cer·i·ty
si·ne cu·ra
si·ne·cure
si·ne die
si·ne pro·le
si·ne qua non
sin·gle
sin·gly
sin·gu·lar
sin·is·ter
sit—down n., adj.
site (location; cf. *cite*,
  sight)
sit·u·ate
sit·u·at·ed
sit·u·a·tion
si·tus
skel·e·ton
slan·der
slan·dered
slan·der·er
slan·der·ous·ly
slaugh·ter

slaugh·tered
slay·ing
sleuth
slight·ed
slight·ing·ly
slip·shod
slov·en·ly
smok·ing
smoth·ered
smoth·er·ing
smug·gle
smug·gler
smug·gling
so·ber
so·bered
so·bri·ety
so·cia·ble
so·cia·bly
so·cial se·cu·ri·ty
so·ci·ety
sol·dier·ly
sole·ly
sol·emn
so·lem·ni·fy
so·lem·ni·ty
sol·em·ni·za·tion
sol·em·nize
sol·emn·ly
so·lic·it
so·lic·i·ta·tion
so·lic·it·ed
so·lic·it·ing
so·lic·i·tor
so·lic·i·tor·ship
so·lic·i·tous·ly
so·lic·i·tous·ness

sol·i·dar·i·ty
sol·i·tary
sol·ven·cy
sol·vent
som·nam·bu·lant
som·nam·bu·lism
som·nam·bu·list
son—in—law
sons—in—law
so·phis·tic
so·phis·ti·cal·ly
so·phis·ti·cate
so·phis·ti·cat·ed
sov·er·eign
sov·er·eign·ty
spasm
spas·mod·ic
spas·tic
spas·tic·i·ty
spe·cial·ly
spe·cial·ty
spe·cie sing.
spe·cies pl.
spe·cif·ic
spe·cif·i·cal·ly
spec·i·fi·ca·tion
spec·i·fic·i·ty
spec·i·fied
spec·i·fy·ing
spec·i·men
spe·cious
spe·cious·ly
spe·cious·ness
spec·u·late
spec·u·lat·ed
spec·u·la·tion

spec·u·la·tive
spec·u·la·tor
spend·thrift
spin·ster·hood
spin·ster·ish
spir·it·ed
spir·it·ous
spo·li·ate
spo·li·a·tion
spo·li·a·tor
spon·sor
spon·sored
spon·sor·ship
spon·ta·ne·ous·ly
spouse
spu·ri·ous·ly
squat·ted
squat·ter
squat·ting
stabbed
stab·ber
stab·bing
sta·bil·i·ty
sta·bi·lize
sta·bi·lized
sta·bi·liz·er
stan·dard·iza·tion
stan·dard·ize
stan·dard·ized
stan·dard·iz·ing
sta·re   de·ci·sis
stat·ed
state·ment
sta·tion
sta·tion·ary
   (immobile)

sta·tion·ery (paper)
sta·tis·tics
stat·us   quo
stat·ute (regulation)
stat·u·to·ry
stealth
stealth·i·ly
stealth·i·ness
stel·lion·a·taire
stel·lion·ate
ster·ile
ste·ril·i·ty
ster·il·iza·tion
ster·il·ize
ster·num
ster·to·rous
stew·ard·ship
still·born
stim·u·late
stim·u·lat·ed
stim·u·la·tion
stim·u·la·tive
stint
sti·pend
sti·pen·di·ary
sti·pi·tal
stip·u·late
stip·u·lat·ed
stip·u·la·tion
stip·u·la·tor
stip·u·la·to·ry
stock·bro·ker
stock·bro·ker·age
stock·hold·er
stock—in—trade
stole

sto·len
stop·page
stor·age
store·house
store·room
stow·age
stow·away n.
stow   away v.
strad·dle
strad·dled
strad·dling
strait·jack·et   or
   straight·jack·et
stran·gle
stran·gler
stran·gling
stran·gu·la·tion
strat·a·gem
strat·e·gy
strick·en
stric·ti   ju·ris
strict·ly
strict·ness
stric·ture
strike·break·er
strike·break·ing
stripped
strip·ping
strong—arm adj., v.
stul·ti·fi·ca·tion
stul·ti·fied
stul·ti·fy·ing
su·abil·i·ty
su·ably
sub·agent
sub·al·tern

sub·al·ter·na·tion
sub·al·ter·nate
sub·con·tract
sub·con·trac·tor
sub·cos·tal
sub·di·vide
sub·di·vid·er
sub·di·vi·sion
sub·ject·ed
sub·jec·tion
sub·jec·tive·ly
sub·jec·tive·ness
sub·jec·tiv·ism
sub·jec·tiv·i·ty
sub ju·di·ce
sub·lease
sub·leased
sub·les·see
sub·les·sor
sub·let
sub·let·ting
sub·lux·a·tion
sub·merge
sub·mer·gence
sub·mis·sion
sub·mis·sive·ly
sub·mis·sive·ness
sub·mit
sub·mit·ted
sub·mit·ting
sub mo·do
sub·mort·gage
sub·or·di·nate
sub·or·di·nate·ly
sub·or·di·nate·ness
sub·or·di·na·tive

sub·orn
sub·or·na·tion
sub·orned
sub·orn·er
sub·orn·ing
sub·poe·na ad
  tes·ti·fi·can·dum
sub·poe·na du·ces
  te·cum
sub·poe·naed
sub·poe·na·ing
sub·poe·nas
sub po·tes·ta·te
sub·ro·gate
sub·ro·gat·ed
sub·ro·ga·tion
sub·ro·gee
sub·scribe
sub·scrib·er
sub·script
sub·scrip·tion
sub·se·quence
sub·se·quent·ly
sub·side
sub·sid·ed
sub·si·dence
sub·sid·iar·ies
sub·sid·iary
sub·si·dy
sub·sist
sub·sis·tence
sub·stance
sub·stan·tial
sub·stan·ti·al·i·ty
sub·stan·tial·ly
sub·stan·tial·ness

sub·stan·ti·ate
sub·stan·ti·at·ed
sub·stan·ti·a·tion
sub·stan·ti·a·tive
sub·stan·tive·ly
sub·sti·tute
sub·sti·tut·ed
sub·sti·tu·tion
sub·sti·tu·tion·ary
sub·ten·an·cy
sub·ten·ant
sub·ter·fuge
sub·tract·ed
sub·trac·tion
sub·ver·sion
sub·ver·sive·ly
sub·ver·sive·ness
suc·ceed·ing
suc·cess
suc·ces·sion·al·ly
suc·ces·sive
suc·ces·sor
suc·cinct·ly
suc·cinct·ness
sue
su·er
suf·fer·able
suf·fer·ably
suf·fer·ance
suf·fered
suf·fer·er
suf·fer·ing·ly
suf·fice
suf·fi·cien·cy
suf·fi·cient·ly
suf·fo·cate

suf·fo·cat·ed
suf·fo·ca·tion
suf·fo·ca·tive
suf·frage
sug·gest·ibil·i·ty
sug·gest·ible
sug·ges·tion
sug·ges·tive·ly
sui·ci·dal
sui·ci·dal·ly
sui·cide
sui ge·ner·is
sui ju·ris
su·ing
suit·abil·i·ty
suit·able
suit·ably
suit·or
sum·ma·ri·ly
sum·ma·rize
sum·ma·ry
sum·ma·tion
sum·ma·tion·al
sum·mon v.
sum·moned
sum·mon·er
sum·mons n., v.
sum·monsed
sum·mon·ses pl. n.
sump·tu·ary
sun·dries pl.
sun·dry sing.
su·per·fi·cial
su·per·fi·ci·al·i·ty
su·per·fi·cial·ly
su·per·flu·ous·ly

su·per·flu·ous·ness
su·per·im·pose
su·per·im·posed
su·per·in·tend
su·per·in·ten·dence
su·per·in·ten·den·cy
su·per·in·ten·dent
su·pe·ri·or
su·pe·ri·or·i·ty
su·pe·ri·or·ly
su·per·sede
su·per·se·de·as
su·per·sed·ed
su·per·sed·er
su·per·sed·ing
su·per·vene
su·per·ve·nience
su·per·ve·nient
su·per·ven·tion
su·per·vise
su·per·vi·sion
su·per·vi·sor
su·per·vi·so·ry
sup·plant·ed
sup·ple·ment
sup·ple·ment·al
sup·ple·men·ta·ry
sup·ple·men·ta·tion
sup·pli·ance
sup·pli·ant
sup·pli·ca·tion
sup·plied
sup·pli·er
sup·ply·ing
sup·port·able
sup·port·ably

sup·port·er
sup·port·ive
sup·pose
sup·pos·ed·ly
sup·po·si·tion
sup·po·si·tion·al
sup·press
sup·pressed
sup·press·ible
sup·press·ing
sup·pres·sion
sup·pres·sive
sup·pres·sor
su·pra dic·tus
su·prem·a·cy
su·preme
sur·cease
sur·charge
sure·ties pl.
sure·ty sing.
sure·ty·ship
sur·face
sur·geon
sur·gery
sur·gi·cal·ly
sur·mise
sur·mised
sur·name
sur·plus
sur·plus·age
sur·pris·al
sur·prise
sur·pris·ing·ly
sur·re·but·tal
sur·re·but·ter
sur·re·join·der

sur·ren·der
sur·ren·dered
sur·ren·der·ee
sur·ren·der·or
sur·rep·ti·tious·ly
sur·rep·ti·tious·ness
sur·ro·gate
sur·round·ed
sur·tax
sur·veil·lance
sur·veil·lant
sur·vey
sur·vey·or
sur·viv·al
sur·vive
sur·vi·vor·ship
sus·cep·ti·bil·i·ty
sus·cep·ti·ble
sus·cep·ti·bly
sus·cep·tive·ness
sus·cep·tiv·i·ty
sus·pect
sus·pect·ed
sus·pend·ed
sus·pend·er
sus·pense·ful
sus·pen·sion
sus·pen·sive·ly
sus·pen·so·ry
sus·pi·cion
sus·pi·cioned
sus·pi·cion·ing
sus·pi·cious
sus·pi·cious·ly
sus·pi·cious·ness
sus·tain

sus·tain·able
sus·tained
sus·tain·er
sus·tain·ing
sus·te·nance
swin·dle
swin·dled
swin·dler
swin·dling
syl·la·bi pl.
syl·la·bus sing.
syl·lo·gism
syl·lo·gist
syl·lo·gis·tic
syl·lo·gis·ti·cal·ly
syl·lo·gize
sym·bol (sign)
sym·boled or
    sym·bolled
sym·bol·ic
sym·bol·i·cal·ly
sym·me·try
sym·pa·thet·ic
sym·pa·thize
sym·pa·thiz·er
sym·pa·thy
syn·chro·nism
syn·chro·nis·tic
syn·chro·ni·za·tion
syn·chro·nize
syn·co·pe
syn·dic
syn·di·cal
syn·di·cal·ism
syn·di·cate
syn·di·cat·ed

syn·di·ca·tion
syn·di·ca·tor
syn·drome
syn·on·y·mous·ly
syn·op·ses pl.
syn·op·sis sing.
syn·op·size
syn·op·tic
syn·op·ti·cal·ly
syph·i·lis
syph·i·lit·ic
sys·tem·at·ic
sys·tem·at·i·cal·ly
sys·to·le
sys·tol·ic

tab·leau sing.
tab·leaux pl.
ta·chom·e·ter
tac·it
tac·it·ly
tac·it·ness
tack·ing
tam·per
tam·pered
tam·per·er
tan·gi·bil·i·ty
tan·gi·ble

tan·gi·bly
tare
tar·iff
tar·sus
tav·ern·er
tax·abil·i·ty
tax·able
tax·a·tion
taxed
tax·er
tax·es
taxi·cab
tax·pay·er
team·ster
tech·ni·cal
tech·ni·cal·i·ty
tech·ni·cal·ly
tele·gram
tele·graph
te·leg·ra·phy
tele·phone
Tele·type
tele·vise
tele·vi·sion
tell·er
tem·per·ance
tem·pest
tem·po·ral·i·ty
tem·po·rar·i·ly
tem·po·rary
tem·pus
ten·an·cy
ten·ant (renter; cf. *tenet*)
ten·ant·able
ten·der

ten·dered
ten·e·ment
te·nen·dum
tene·re
te·net (doctrine; cf. *tenant*)
ten·or
ten·ta·tive·ly
ten·ta·tive·ness
ten·u·ous
ten·u·ous·ly
ten·u·ous·ness
ten·ure
ten·ur·ial·ly
ter·mi·na·ble
ter·mi·na·bly
ter·mi·nal
ter·mi·nate
ter·mi·na·ted
ter·mi·na·tion
ter·mi·na·tive·ly
ter·mi·na·tor
ter·mi·ni *or* ter·mi·nus·es (sing.: *terminus*)
ter·mi·no·log·i·cal
ter·mi·nol·o·gy
ter·mi·nus (pl.: *termi-ni* or *terminuses*)
ter·mi·nus a quo
ter·ri·to·ri·al·ly
ter·ri·to·ry
test·able
tes·ta·cy
tes·ta·ment
tes·ta·men·ta·ry

tes·tate
tes·ta·tion
tes·ta·tor mas.
tes·ta·trix fem.
tes·ta·tum
tes·ti·fied
tes·ti·fy
tes·ti·fy·ing
tes·ti·mo·ni·al
tes·ti·mo·ni·um
tes·ti·mo·ny
tex·tu·al
theft·proof
thence·forth
thence·for·ward
the·o·ry
ther·a·py
there·abouts *or* there·about
there·af·ter
there·at
there·by
there·for (in return for)
there·fore (consequently)
there·from
there·in
there·in·af·ter
there·of
there·on
there·to
there·to·fore
there·un·der
there·upon
there·with

101

thief sing.
thieve v.
thiev·ery
thieves pl.
thiev·ish·ness
tho·rac·ic
tho·rax
thor·ough·fare
threat·en
threat·ened
threat·en·er
threat·en·ing·ly
throm·bo·sis
throm·bus
tib·ia
tick·et·ed
tid·al
tid·al·ly
tide·lands
tide·wa·ter
tide·way
tim·ber
tim·bered
tip—off n.
tip off v.
tip·staff
tip·ster
tis·sue
ti·tle
ti·tled
ti·tling
to·geth·er·ness
to·ken
tol·er·ance
tol·er·ant·ly
tol·er·ate

tol·er·at·ed
toll·age
toll·booth
ton·nage
ton·tine
tort (wrongful act)
tort·feas·or
tor·tious (involving tort)
tor·tu·ous (winding)
tor·ture
tor·tured
tor·tur·er
to·tal
to·taled or to·talled
to·tal·ing or to·tal·ling
to·tum
tour·ist
tow·age
to·ward
town·ship
tox·emia
tox·ic
tox·i·cant
tox·ic·i·ty
tox·i·co·log·ic
tox·i·co·log·i·cal·ly
tox·i·col·o·gist
tox·i·col·o·gy
tox·i·co·sis
tra·che·al
tra·che·ot·o·my
trade·mark
trade name

trade se·cret
trades·man
tra·di·tion·al·ism
tra·di·tion·al·ist
tra·di·tion·al·is·tic
tra·di·tion·al·ly
tra·di·tion·ary
traf·fic
traf·ficked
traf·fick·er
traf·fick·ing
trag·e·dy
trail·er
trai·tor·ous·ly
tran·quil
tran·quil·li·ty
trans·act·ed
trans·ac·tion
trans·ac·tor
tran·script
tran·scrip·tion
trans·fer
trans·fer·able
trans·fer·al
trans·fer·ee
trans·fer·or
trans·ferred
trans·fer·rer
trans·fer·ring
tran·sience
tran·sien·cy
tran·sient
tran·sient·ly
tran·sit
tran·si·tion·al
tran·si·to·ry

trans·lat·abil·i·ty
trans·lat·able
trans·late
trans·lat·ed
trans·la·tion
trans·la·tive
trans·la·tor
trans·mis·sion
trans·mis·sive
trans·mis·siv·i·ty
trans·mit
trans·mit·ta·ble
trans·mit·tal
trans·mit·tance
trans·mit·ted
trans·mit·ter
trans·mit·ting
tran·spire
tran·spired
trans·port·abil·i·ty
trans·port·able
trans·por·ta·tion
trans·por·ta·tion·al
trans·port·ed
trans·verse
trau·ma
trau·mat·ic
trau·mat·i·cal·ly
trau·ma·tism
trau·ma·tize
trav·eled   *or*
   trav·elled
trav·el·er   *or*
   trav·el·ler
trav·el·ing   *or*
   trav·el·ling

tra·vers·able
tra·vers·al
tra·verse
tra·versed
tra·vers·er
treach·er·ous·ly
treach·er·ous·ness
treach·ery
trea·son
trea·son·able
trea·son·ably
trea·son·ous
trea·sure
trea·sured
trea·sur·er
trea·sury
trea·ties
treat·ment
trea·ty
trem·or
tres·pass
tres·passed
tres·pass·er
tres·pass·ing
tri·al
tri·bu·nal
trib·u·tar·ies
trib·u·tary
tried
tri·er
tri·par·tite
tri·par·ti·tion
trip·li·cate
trip·li·ca·tion
triv·ia
triv·i·al

triv·i·al·i·ty
triv·i·al·ly
tro·chan·ter
tro·ver
trust   cor·pus
trust·ed
trust·ee
trust·ee·ing
trust·ees
trust·ee·ship
trus·ter
trust·ing
truth·ful·ly
try·ing·ly
tu·ber·os·i·ty
tu·ition
tur·moil
turn·key
turn   out v.
turn·out n.
turn·pike
turn·ta·ble
tur·pi·tude
tu·te·lage
tu·te·lary
tu·tor·age
tu·tored
tu·tor·ship
twist·ed
twist·ing
ty·po·graph·i·cal
ty·ran·ni·cal
tyr·an·nize
tyr·an·nous
tyr·an·ny
ty·rant

103

uber·ri·ma fi·des
ubiq·ui·tous·ly
ubiq·ui·tous·ness
ubiq·ui·ty
ubi re ve·ra
ubi su·pra
ul·cer
ul·cer·at·ed
ul·cer·a·tive
ul·lage
ul·na
ul·te·ri·or
ul·ti·ma ra·tio
ul·ti·mate
ul·ti·mate·ly
ul·ti·ma·tum sing.
ul·ti·ma·tums or
  ul·ti·ma·ta pl.
ul·tra vi·res
um·brage
um·pire
un·abat·ed
un·ab·solved
un·ac·ces·si·ble
un·ac·count·able
un·ac·cred·it·ed
un·ac·crued
un·ac·cused
un·ad·just·ed
un·ad·vised

un·ad·vis·ed·ly
un·ag·gres·sive-
  ness
un·alien·able
un·alien·at·ed
un·al·low·able
un·al·ter·able
un·al·tered
un·am·big·u·ous·ly
una·nim·i·ty
unan·i·mous·ly
un·an·swer·able
un·an·swered
un·ap·peal·able
un·ap·peas·able
un·ap·peased
un·ap·pre·hen·sive
un·apt
un·ar·gu·able
un·armed
un·ar·rest·ed
un·as·cer·tain·able
un·as·sailed
un·as·sign·able
un·as·signed
un·as·suage·able
un·au·tho·rized
un·avail·able
un·avenged
un·avoid·abil·i·ty
un·avoid·able
un·avoid·ably
un·aware
un·bail·able
un·bal·anced
un·bear·able

un·be·com·ing
un·be·fit·ting
un·be·known
un·ben·e·fi·cial
un·be·queathed
un·bi·ased
un·blem·ished
un·bro·ken
un·ceas·ing·ly
un·cen·sored
un·cer·tain·ties
un·cer·tain·ty
un·con·di·tion·al·ly
un·con·di·tioned
un·con·fessed
un·con·scio·na·ble
un·con·scio·na·bly
un·con·scious
un·con·sti·tu·tion·al
un·con·strained
un·con·test·able
un·con·test·ed
un·con·trol·la·ble
un·con·trolled
un·con·tro·vert·ed
un·con·tro·vert·ible
un·cum·bered
un·dam·aged
un·de·cid·ed
un·de·fend·able
un·de·fend·ed
un·de·fined
un·de·lib·er·ate
un·dem·o·crat·ic
un·de·mon·stra·ble
un·dem·on·strat·ed

un·de·mon·stra·tive
un·de·ni·a·ble
un·de·ni·a·bly
un·de·nied
un·de·pend·a·ble
un·der·charge
un·der·charged
un·der·es·ti·mate
un·der·es·ti·mat·ed
un·der·es·ti·ma·tion
un·der·go
un·der·gone
un·der·ground
un·der·hand·ed·ly
un·der·in·sure
un·der·in·sured
un·der·lease
un·der·les·see
un·der·mine
un·der·pay·ment
un·der·priv·i·leged
un·der·sher·iff
un·der·signed
un·der·stand·a·ble
un·der·stand·ing
un·der·state
un·der·stat·ed
un·der·state·ment
un·der·stood
un·der·take
un·der·tak·en
un·der·tak·er
un·der·tak·ing
un·der·ten·ant
un·der·took
un·der·val·u·a·tion

un·der·value
un·der·write
un·der·writ·er
un·der·writ·ing
un·der·writ·ten
un·der·wrote
un·de·served
un·des·ig·nat·ed
un·de·sir·a·bil·i·ty
un·de·sir·a·ble
un·de·spoiled
un·de·tect·a·ble
un·de·tect·ed
un·dis·cern·ing
un·dis·ci·plined
un·dis·closed
un·dis·cov·er·a·ble
un·dis·cov·ered
un·dis·guis·a·ble
un·dis·guised
un·dis·put·a·ble
un·dis·put·ed
un·di·vid·ed
un·di·vulged
un·doc·u·ment·a·ble
un·doc·u·ment·ed
un·due
un·du·ly
un·earned
un·eas·i·ly
un·eas·i·ness
un·easy
un·ed·u·cat·ed
un·emo·tion·al
un·em·ploy·a·bil·i·ty
un·em·ploy·a·ble

un·em·ployed
un·em·ploy·ment
un·en·dorsed
un·en·force·a·ble
un·en·forced
un·en·tailed
un·equaled
un·equal·ly
un·equiv·o·cal·ly
un·err·ing
un·es·cap·a·ble
un·es·sen·tial
un·eth·i·cal
un·ex·cep·tion·a·ble
un·ex·e·cut·ed
un·ex·pect·ed
un·ex·pired
un·fair·ly
un·fair·ness
un·faith·ful
un·fa·mil·iar
un·fa·vor·a·ble
un·fin·ished
un·fit·ness
un·fo·ren·sic
un·fore·seen
un·for·giv·a·ble
un·for·tu·nate·ly
un·found·ed·ly
un·friend·ly
un·ful·filled
un·gov·ern·a·ble
un·guar·an·teed
un·guard·ed
un·guilty
un·ham·pered

un·harmed
un·heed·ful
un·hes·i·tat·ing·ly
un·iden·ti·fi·able
un·iden·ti·fied
uni·fi·ca·tion
uni·fied
uni·form
uni·for·mi·ty
uni·form·ly
un·i·form·ness
uni·fy
uni·lat·er·al·ly
un·im·paired
un·im·peach·able
un·im·peached
un·im·ped·ed
un·im·proved
un·in·cor·po·rat·ed
un·in·fect·ed
un·in·hib·it·ed
un·in·jured
un·in·spect·ed
un·in·sur·able
un·in·sured
un·in·tel·li·gi·bil·i·ty
un·in·tel·li·gi·ble
un·in·tel·li·gi·bly
un·in·ten·tion·al
un·in·ter·rupt·ed
union
union·ized
un·is·sued
unite
unit·ed
unit·ed·ly

unit·er
unit·ing
uni·ty
uni·ver·sal
uni·ver·sal·i·ty
uni·ver·sal·ly
uni·ver·si·tas
   ju·ris
uni·ver·si·tas
   re·rum
un·ju·di·cial
un·ju·di·cious
un·just
un·jus·ti·fi·able
un·jus·ti·fied
un·just·ly
un·just·ness
un·know·ing·ly
un·known
un·law·ful
un·law·ful·ly
un·law·ful·ness
un·like·li·hood
un·lim·it·ed
un·liq·ui·dat·ed
un·man·age·able
un·mar·ket·able
un·mar·ried
un·med·i·tat·ed
un·mind·ful
un·mis·tak·able
un·mo·lest·ed
un·mor·al
un·nat·u·ral
un·nec·es·sar·i·ly
un·nec·es·sary

un·ob·jec·tion·able
un·ob·scured
un·ob·served
un·ob·struct·ed
un·ob·tain·able
un·oc·cu·pied
un·of·fi·cial
un·op·pressed
un·op·pres·sive
un·or·tho·dox
un·paid
un·par·al·leled
un·pat·ent·ed
un·peace·able
un·per·ceived
un·pleas·ant·ness
un·pol·lut·ed
un·pre·ce·dent·ed·ly
un·prej·u·diced
un·pre·med·i·tat·ed
un·pre·vent·able
un·prin·ci·pled
un·print·able
un·pro·fes·sion·al
un·pro·tect·ed
un·pro·test·ed
un·prov·able
un·pro·voked
un·pun·ished
un·qual·i·fied
un·ques·tion·able
un·ques·tioned
un·rav·el
un·rav·el·ing
un·rea·son·able-
   ness

un·rea·son·ably
un·rec·og·niz·able
un·rec·on·cil·able
un·rec·on·ciled
un·re·deem·able
un·re·form·able
un·re·fut·ed
un·reg·is·tered
un·re·lat·ed
un·re·lent·ing
un·re·li·abil·ity
un·re·li·able
un·re·morse·ful
un·re·pealed
un·re·pent·ant
un·re·port·ed
un·re·quit·able
un·re·solv·able
un·re·solved
un·re·spon·sive
un·re·strained
un·re·strict·ed·ly
un·re·vealed
un·re·voked
un·ruly
un·safe
un·sal·able
un·sanc·tioned
un·san·i·tary
un·sa·vory
un·se·cured
un·seg·re·gat·ed
un·sen·tenced
un·so·lic·it·ed
un·sound·ly
un·stead·i·ly

un·sub·si·dized
un·sub·stan·ti·at·ed
un·suit·abil·i·ty
un·suit·able
un·sul·lied
un·sus·pect·ed
un·sus·pi·cious
un·sym·pa·thet·ic
un·tar·nished
un·ten·a·bil·i·ty
un·ten·a·ble
un·til
un·to·ward
un·trace·able
un·trans·fer·able
un·true
un·trust·wor·thi-
   ness
un·trust·wor·thy
un·usu·al
un·usu·al·ly
un·usu·al·ness
un·ver·i·fi·able
un·ver·i·fied
un·vin·dic·tive
un·war·i·ness
un·war·rant·ed·ly
un·wary
un·wel·come
un·whole·some
un·wit·ness·ed
un·wit·ting·ly
un·wor·thi·ness
un·wor·thy
un·writ·ten
un·zoned

up·keep
up·lands
ur·ban·iza·tion
ure·mia
us·age
used
use·ful·ness
us·er
usu·al·ly
usu·fruct
usu·fruc·tu·ary
usu·ri·ous
usu·ri·ous·ly
usu·ri·ous·ness
usurp
usur·pa·tion
usurped
usurp·er
usu·ry
ut
uten·sil
uter·ine
util·i·tar·i·an
util·i·ties
util·i·ty
uti·li·za·tion
uti·lize
uti·lized
uti·liz·er
uti·liz·ing
uti pos·si·de·tis
ut·most
ut·ru·bi
ut·ter
ut·ter·able
ut·ter·ance

ut·tered
ut·ter·ly
ut·ter·most
ux·or
ux·or·i·cide

va·can·cy
va·cant
va·can·tia   bo·na
va·cant·ly
va·cate
va·cat·ed
va·cat·ing
va·ca·tion
va·ca·tur
vac·ci·na·tion
va·cu·ity
vac·u·um
vag·a·bond·age
va·gran·cy
va·grant
vague·ly
vague·ness
val·id
val·i·date
val·i·dat·ed
val·i·dat·ing
val·i·da·tion

va·lid·i·ty
val·id·ly
valu·able
valu·able·ness
valu·ably
val·u·a·tion·al
val·u·a·tor
val·ue·less
val·u·er
val·u·ing
van·dal
van·dal·ism
van·dal·is·tic
van·dal·ize
van·dal·ized
van·dal·iz·ing
va·ra
vari·ance
vari·ant
vari·a·tion
var·ied
va·ri·e·ty
var·i·ous
vary·ing
vas   sing.
va·sa   pl.
vas·cu·lar
vault
ve·hi·cle
ve·hic·u·lar
ve·jours
vel   non
ve·nal
ve·nal·i·ty
ve·nal·ly
vend·ed

vend·ee
vend·er   or
   ven·dor
vend·ibil·ity
vend·ible   or
   vend·able
vend·ing
ven·di·tion
ven·di·tioni
   ex·pon·as
ven·due
ven·er·abil·i·ty
ven·er·able
ve·ne·re·al
ven·geance
venge·ful·ly
ve·ni·re   fa·ci·as
   de   no·vo
ve·nire·man
ve·nous
ven·tral
ven·tri·cle
ven·tric·u·lar
ven·ture
ven·tured
ven·ue
ve·ra·cious·ly
ve·ra·cious   ness
ve·rac·i·ties
ve·rac·i·ty
ver·bal·ism
ver·bal·iza·tion
ver·bal·ize
ver·bal·ly
ver·ba·tim
ver·biage

108

ver·bose
ver·dict
ver·i·fi·abil·i·ty
ver·i·fi·able
ver·i·fi·ca·tion
ver·i·fied
ver·i·fi·er
ver·i·fy
ver·i·fy·ing
ver·i·ly
ver·i·ty
ver·sa·tile
ver·sa·til·i·ty
ver·sus
ver·te·bra sing.
ver·te·brae or
   ver·te·bras pl.
ver·te·bral
ver·ti·go
vest·ed
ves·tige
vet·er·an
vet·er·i·nar·i·an
ve·to
ve·toed
ve·to·er
ve·toes
vex·a·tion
vex·a·tious·ly
vex·a·tious·ness
via
vi·a·bil·i·ty
vi·a·ble
vi·car·i·ous·ly
vi·car·i·ous·ness
vice—prin·ci·pal adj.

vice   squad
vice   ver·sa
vice—war·den
vic·i·nage
vic·i·nal
vi·cin·i·ty
vi·cious·ly
vi·cious·ness
vi·cis·si·tude
vic·tim·ize
vic·tim·ized
vic·tim·iz·ing
vict·uals
vi·de
vi·de·li·cet
vi·di·mus
vi   et   armis
vig·i·lance
vig·i·lant adj.
vig·i·lan·te n.
vig·or·ous·ly
vig·or·ous·ness
vil·i·fi·ca·tion
vil·i·fied
vil·i·fi·er
vil·i·fy
vil·i·fy·ing
vil·lage
vil·lain
vil·lain·ous·ly
vil·lainy
vin·di·cate
vin·di·cat·ed
vin·di·ca·tion
vin·di·ca·to·ry
vin·dic·tive·ly

vin·dic·tive·ness
vi·o·late
vi·o·lat·ed
vi·o·la·tion
vi·o·la·tor
vi·o·lence
vi·o·lent·ly
vi·o·lent·ness
vir·tu·al·ly
vir·tue
vir·tu·ous·ly
vir·tu·ous·ness
vir·u·lent
vi·sa
vis—à—vis
vis·cera
vis·cer·al
vis·i·bil·i·ty
vis·i·ble
vis·i·bly
vis·it
vis·i·ta·tion
vis·i·tor
vis   ma·jor
vis·u·al·ize
vi·ta
vi·tal
vi·tal·i·ty
vi·tal·ly
vi·ti·ate
vi·ti·at·ed
vi·ti·a·tion
vi·ti·a·tor
vi·tu·per·a·tion
vi·tu·per·a·tive
vi·va   vo·ce

viz. (abbreviation of
videlicet)
vo·ca·tion (career; cf.
avocation)
vo·cif·er·ous·ly
void·able
void·ed
voir dire
vo·len·ti non
fit in·jur·ia
vo·li·tion
vol·ley
vol·un·tar·i·ly
vol·un·tary
vol·un·teer
vouch
vouched
vouch·er
vul·gar
vul·gar·i·ty
vul·gar·ly
vul·ner·a·bil·i·ty
vul·ner·a·ble

wa·ger
wa·gered
waif n.
waive v.
waived

waiv·er
waiv·ing
wan·ton·ly
wan·ton·ness
war·den·ship
warn·ing
war·rant
war·rant·ed
war·ran·tee (person;
cf. *warranty*)
war·ran·ties (sing.:
warranty)
war·rant·ing
war·ran·to
war·ran·tor
war·ran·ty
(agreement; cf.
warrantee)
watch·man
wa·tered
wa·ter·line
wa·ter·mark
wa·ter·way
way·bill
weap·on
weap·on·less
wed·lock
weir
wel·fare
when·so·ev·er
where·af·ter
where·as
where·by
where·fore
where·in
where·of

where·up·on
wheth·er
whip·lash
whole (entire)
whol·ly
wid·ow
wid·owed
wid·ow·er
wild·cat·ter
will·ful *or*
wil·ful
will·ful·ly
will·full·ness
will·ing·ly
wind·storm
wind·up n.
wind up v.
with·draw
with·draw·al
with·drawn
with·drew
with·held
with·hold
with·stand·ing
wit·ness
wit·nessed
wit·ness·es
wit·ting·ly
work·man·like
work·man·ship
work·men
work·shop
wor·thi·ness
worth·less·ly
wor·thy
wound·ed

wran·gle
wran·gled
wran·gling
wreck·age
wrecked
wreck·er
writ
write—off n.
write off v.
wrong·do·ing
wrong·ful
wrong·ful·ly
wrong·ful·ness

yel·low—dog adj.
yield
yield·ed
yield·ing

X ray n.
X—ray adj., v.
Xe·rox

Z

zeal·ous·ly
zig·zag
zoned
zon·ing
zy·go·ma
zy·go·mat·ic

Reference Section

The rules for punctuation discussed and illustrated in this reference section are in general agreement with those in the *Reference Manual for Stenographers and Typists, Fourth Edition.** Since the presentation here deals only with the most common problems in writing or typing legal correspondence and other papers, a complete general source such as the *Reference Manual* or a technical reference such as the *Legal Secretary's Complete Handbook†* should be consulted for help with special problems.

Using punctuation to help convey meaning correctly and clearly is of particular importance in legal work. The following summary of the comma, semicolon, and other rules will help you solve the vast majority of punctuation problems.

COMMA

Comma After Introductory Expression. Use a comma after an introductory clause. The word that introduces such a clause may be a relative pronoun (*that, who, what, which, whoever, whatever, whichever*) or a subordinating conjunction (*if, when, though, although, whether, unless, as, because, since, while, where, after, wherever, until, before, how, however*).

> Whichever course of action you decide to take, we will support you in every way we can.
>
> If nothing is done about it prior to December 27 of this year, the Judge will be powerless to reduce the fine imposed.

*Ruth E. Gavin and William A. Sabin, *Reference Manual for Stenographers and Typists,* 4th ed., Gregg Division, McGraw-Hill Book Company, New York, 1970.

†Besse May Miller, *Legal Secretary's Complete Handbook,* Prentice-Hall, Inc., Englewood Cliffs, N.J., 1953.

Also use a comma after an introductory phrase containing a verb form.

> Having just received a telephone call from the Clerk of the Federal District Court, I am writing to inform you that the Judge denied the motion to vacate or reduce the fine imposed.

Too, use a comma after *for instance, in brief, on the contrary, for example,* or a similar introductory expression.

> In brief, I believe it would be to your advantage to settle the matter out of court.

Comma With Nonrestrictive Expression. Use commas to set off nonstrictive clauses and phrases, which are expressions that can be omitted without changing the meaning of the sentences in which they appear. If the clause or phrase is restrictive (essential to identify, define, or restrict the meaning of the noun it modifies), do not use commas to set it off from the rest of the sentence.

> *Restrictive—no commas:* Please send me a doctor's certificate that outlines the extent of your disability.
>
> *Nonrestrictive—commas:* Enclosed is a computation of what the Department considers to be your civil liability for tax, which is entirely separate from any criminal phase.

Although careful writers use *that* to introduce a restrictive clause and *which* to introduce a nonrestrictive clause, many writers use *that* and *which* interchangeably. Therefore, the secretary or typist must be very alert to punctuate according to the writer's intended meaning.

Punctuating phrases correctly requires careful attention too. Again, the writer's intended meaning is the key to correct punctuation.

> *Restrictive—no commas:* The settlement agreed to by both parties on March 11 still has not been made.
>
> *Nonrestrictive—commas:* The settlement, agreed to by both parties on March 11, still has not been made.

In the first sentence *agreed to by both parties on March 11* was intended to identify or define a specific settlement; therefore, no commas were used. Perhaps because only one settlement had been mutually agreed to, the writer of the second sentence above felt that *agreed to by both parties on March 11* was not necessary; therefore, it is set off with commas.

Comma With Parenthetical Expression. Simply to make his meaning clearer, a writer sometimes inserts a comment or an explanation that could be omitted without changing the meaning of the sentence. Such comments and explanations are called *parenthetical expressions,* and they are always set off with commas, parentheses, or dashes. Ordinarily, commas are preferable.

> The Government, I can see, naturally feels that they have a good case.

Comma With Name in Direct Address. Use commas to set off a name used in direct address.

> This letter, Mr. Landers, is in the nature of a report to you of the conference that I had in Washington yesterday.

Comma With Appositive. A writer sometimes mentions a certain person or thing and then, in order to make his meaning perfectly clear, says the same thing in different words (uses an appositive). If the appositive occurs within the sentence, use two commas to set it off.

> The foreman of the jury, Mr. Davis, seemed to pay little attention to the testimony of several witnesses.

If the appositive comes at the end of the sentence, use only one comma to set it off.

> The hearing is scheduled for next Friday, April 24.

Comma in Series. When three or more similar expressions (words, phrases, or clauses) appear in a series with a conjunction (*and, or, nor,* for example) before the last expression, use a comma after each expression except the last one.

> We could meet with you anytime next Monday, Tuesday, or Friday.
> Mr. Finch, Miss Helms, and Mr. Morris will be happy to assist you.

Comma to Indicate Omission of "And." Instead of being joined by *and,* two adjectives preceding a noun usually are separated by a comma.

> A long, complicated Stipulation of Facts was agreed upon by the opposing attorneys.

However, do not use a comma if the first adjective modifies the combined idea of the second adjective and the noun.

> A complete medical report was requested by the insurance company's lawyers.

Comma to Indicate Omission of Understood Words. Use a comma to indicate the omission of one or more important words that can be understood from the context.

> A payment of $1,000 on the attorney's fee is due before the trial; the remainder, to be secured by a note signed by you and Mrs. Landers.

Comma With Contrasted Expression. Use commas to set off an expression that is in contrast with some other expression in the sentence.

> A good witness states only the facts, not hearsay evidence, at all times.

Always be sure to set off the complete contrasting expression, not just part of it.

> The doctor's certificate must indicate that your indisposition originates from a physical, not a mental, cause.

Comma With Quotation. Use commas to set off a short complete quotation from the rest of the sentence.

> An earlier letter from his lawyer stated, ''We are requesting separate trials in the matters of tax evasion and mail fraud.''
>
> ''We are requesting separate trials in the matters of tax evasion and mail fraud,'' an earlier letter from his lawyer stated.
>
> ''We,'' an earlier letter from his lawyer stated, ''are requesting separate trials in the matters of tax evasion and mail fraud.''

Comma in an Address. Within a sentence, use a comma to separate the parts of an address.

> This letter is to confirm our telephone conversation regarding the communication I received from the Regional Counsel of the Internal Revenue Service in Boston, Massachusetts, concerning the Stipulation of Facts.
>
> I believe that 1110 West 90 Street, New York, New York 10025, is his home address.

As illustrated in the second sentence above, do not use a comma to separate the state and the ZIP Code.

Comma in a Date. Always use a comma to separate the day from the year or, when the day is omitted, the month from the year. Within a sentence, also use a comma after the year.

> The petitioner's counsel has been unable to contact him since November 16, 1971.
>
> The agreement was signed on March 14, 1970, according to our records.
>
> In June, 1970, we met with Mr. Young on several occasions.

Comma Between Independent Clauses. Use a comma to separate the independent clauses joined by *and, but, or,* or *nor.* (Also see the semicolon rules on page 117.)

> I would appreciate an immediate reply to this letter, but in the meantime I will attempt to contact the Regional Office in Boston.

SEMICOLON

Semicolon Between Independent Clauses. If the independent clauses are not joined by *and, but, or,* or *nor,* use a semicolon between them.

> I have a copy of Mr. Smith's will; the original is in the safe at his home.

If the independent clauses are joined by *accordingly, however, nevertheless, consequently,* or some other conjunctive adverb, use a semicolon before and a comma after the conjunctive adverb.

> The Judge has agreed to your serving with me as coexecutor; consequently, I am enclosing for your signature the necessary papers to initiate probate of this estate.

If the independent clauses are connected by *and* or some other coordinating conjunction and if one of the clauses contains a comma, use a semicolon before the conjunction joining the clauses if using a comma might cause confusion or misinterpretation in reading.

> He has been interviewed by Mr. Paulson, Mr. Norris; and Mr. Paulson's associate, Mr. Wilson, would like to see him next Tuesday.

Semicolon in Series. If one or more of the items in a series is punctuated with commas, use a semicolon to separate the items.

> The Petitioner, John Powers, is seventy-five years old; his health has been failing; and communications between counsel and said Petitioner have been impaired.

Semicolon Before Introductory Expression. If an illustration, a list, or an explanation is added almost as an afterthought at the end of a sentence, use a semicolon before and a comma after *for example, that is, namely, for instance,* or other introductory expression.

I discussed a very important matter with the Judge; namely, the method of accomplishing the settlement of the John Hope Trust in accordance with the decree of the Superior Court.

COLON

Colon Before Introductory Expression. If the first part of a sentence suggests that an illustration, a list, or an explanation follows, use a colon before and a comma after *for example, that is, namely, for instance,* or other introductory expression.

The Defendant intends to file with this Honorable Court an Amended Motion to Dismiss and a Memorandum of Law, in the light of three decisions of the Supreme Court of the United States: namely, *Marchetti* v. *United States,* 36 LW 4143 (January 29, 1968); *Grosso* v. *United States,* 36 LW 4150 (January 29, 1968); and *Haynes* v. *United States,* 36 LW 4164 (January 29, 1968).

Colon After Introductory Expression. Use a colon after an expression or statement that introduces a long quotation, an explanatory or illustrative clause, or a list or series of items not introduced by *for example, that is,* or a similar expression.

I am enclosing the following dividends for deposit in the estate of Kenneth L. Fox: Texaco, Inc., $50; Merck & Co., Inc., $40; and Union Carbide Corporation, $110.

This leaves only one alternative: you must pay the fine or be placed in the custody of the authorities.

QUOTATIONS

Complete Quotation. Use quotation marks to enclose a complete direct quotation, that is, the exact words spoken or written by someone else. Use a comma to introduce a short quotation and a colon to introduce a long quotation.

Federal Rules Civil Procedure 9 (B) states, ''Circumstances instituting fraud shall be stated with particularity.''

In Volume 13 of *American Jurisprudence* at page 192, Section 48, we find: ''A bona fide attempt to organize a corporation under a valid existing statute authorizing the creation of a corporation such as that attempted to be created will result in the creation of a corporation de facto . . . *the existence of which can be called into question only by the state in a direct proceeding for that purpose.*" (Italics supplied.)

Incomplete Quotation. Use quotation marks to enclose only the word or words that are part of a direct quotation.

> The testimony also brought out that his wife, Mary Landers, "has been involuntarily made a joint Petitioner in this matter."

Lengthy Quotation. A lengthy quotation in a legal document is usually single-spaced and may be handled in either of these ways:

1. Type a quotation mark at the beginning of each quoted paragraph, but use a closing quotation mark only at the end of the last quoted paragraph. Use single quotation marks (apostrophes) to enclose any quotations within the quotation.
2. Reset the left margin five spaces to the right of the original margin, and indent the first line of the paragraph five additional spaces. Reset the right margin five spaces to the left of the original margin. Omit the opening and closing quotation marks. In this style, use regular quotation marks for any quotations within the quoted material.

Other Quotations. Use quotation marks to enclose the following: words referred to as words (also see rules for underscoring and italicizing); misnomers; slang; words used in a sense different from the ordinary meaning; titles of legal documents when introduced by the word *entitled;* titles of magazine articles; titles of unpublished manuscripts.

> The document entitled "Indenture of Trust" set forth the agreement or contract entered into by Ralph Powers and the New England Trust Company.
>
> Numerous so-called "relatives" appeared when the Will could not be found.

Order of Quotation With Other Punctuation Marks.   Always
type the comma and the period inside the closing quotation
mark; type the colon and semicolon outside the closing
quotation mark. Place other punctuation marks inside or
outside the closing quotation mark, according to the sense of
the sentence.

> "The Trustee," the Indenture of Trust specifically stated, "shall
> have full power and authority to sell and convert into money the
> whole or any part of said Trust Estate."
>
> The papers were clearly marked "Rush"; however, they were not
> sent by airmail.
>
> Does the Will answer my question, "What is to become of the
> lake property"?
>
> The Will answers my original question, "What is to become of
> the lake property?"

Omissions in Quotations.   In quoted matter use three periods, with a space before and after each period, to show the
omission of words within or at the beginning of a sentence. To
show an omission at the end of a sentence that would end with
a period, use four spaced periods.

To show the omission of one or more paragraphs, type three
spaced asterisks on a line by themselves. Center the asterisks.

* * *

BRACKETS

Brackets in Quotations.   Use brackets to enclose the word
sic when it is used to show that an error has been recognized
but not changed in quoted material. The expression *sic*
immediately follows the words or figures that have been
reproduced exactly from the original.

> "There were two [sic] children born of this marriage; namely,
> Susan, David, and James Lawrence."

Use brackets to enclose a correction or explanation made by someone other than the person quoted.

> His letter said, "The mortgage on the so-called Eastman property [owned by George W. Brown] is still undischarged, and the balance due is $l,500."

UNDERSCORE AND ITALICS

Use underscores as a substitute for italics in typed material or to indicate what is to be italicized in printed material.

Names of Cases. Underscore the names of cases—except the *v.* or *vs.,* which stands for *versus*—when used in the body of correspondence or documents.

> He cited the case of Smith v. Jones et al.

Foreign Words and Phrases. Underscore foreign words and phrases that have not become part of the English language.

> capias   a fortiori   nolo contendere   supra

Titles of Publications. Underscore the names of books, magazines, and newspapers.

> The Manual for the Legal Secretarial Profession was prepared by the National Association of Legal Secretaries.

Emphasis. Underscore words, phrases, clauses, or sentences to give them greater prominence or emphasis.

> Should the libelant move within 10 miles of town, the libelee agrees to pay the reasonable costs of moving—limited to one move only.

HYPHEN

Hyphen in Compound Adjective. Use a hyphen between the parts of a compound adjective preceding the noun it modifies.

> Mr. Adams is a well-known lawyer.

However, a two-word proper name used as an adjective is not hyphenated, nor is a modifier that contains an adverb ending in *ly*.

> According to our New York office, he controls several privately owned corporations.

If the modifier consists of a number or letter plus *room, acre, foot, inch, shaped, frame,* or some other word, use a hyphen between the number or letter and the following word.

> 40-acre plot   L-shaped scar   A-frame house   12-page report

Hyphen in Other Compound Words.   Use a hyphen to join the parts of a constructed verb, a constructed noun containing a preposition, an "improvised" word, or a compound number below one hundred.

> *Verbs:* blue-pencil   cross-license   double-check
> *Nouns:* right-of-way   mother-in-law   patent-in-fee
> *Improvised words:* know-how   know-it-all
> *Compound numbers:* twenty-one   eighty-nine

The best procedure to follow when writing compound words is to consult the dictionary. If the word is shown, follow the dictionary style regardless of the rules stated here.

Hyphen After Prefix.   When adding *ex, pro, un, anti,* or a similar prefix to a proper noun or proper adjective, use a hyphen after the prefix.

> ex-President   pro-British   un-American   anti-Communist

Use a hyphen to join duplicated prefixes.

> re-redirect examination   sub-subcommittee

Suspended, or Spaced, Hyphen.   Use a hyphen followed by a space when two or more hyphenated compounds have a common basic element.

> long- and short-term notes   five- or six-page report